MW00911989

The Soul Fast Work

By: Cassandra Mack

Hi Deanne
all the best
Cassandra M

The Soul Fast Workbook

Copyright © 2017 by Cassandra Mack. All rights reserved.

This book, or parts thereof, may not be reproduced in any form without the author's permission, except in the case of brief quotations embodied in critical articles or reviews. The scanning, uploading, and distribution of this book via the Internet or any other means without the permission of the publisher is illegal and punishable by law. Please purchase only authorized electronic editions, and do not participate in or encourage piracy of copyrighted materials. Your support of the author's rights is appreciated.

All scripture quotations are taken from The Holy Bible, King James Version (KJV), the Holy Bible English Standard Version (ESV) and the Holy Bible New International Version (NIV).

Printed in the U.S.A. by Morris Publishing ®
3212 E Hwy 30
Kearney, NE 68847
800-650-7888

ISBN: 978-0-9718728-0-6

Published by: Strategies for Empowered Living Inc.
StrategiesForEmpoweredLiving.com

Join Us By Phone
From The Comfort of Your Home
You're Invited To
Church By Phone

Sunday Morning Hour of Power

Be Part of The Growing Conversation
With Cassandra Mack
& People of Faith From All Around The Globe

1-712-432-3066
Code 740332

Sundays
8:45 AM (EST) 7:45 AM (CST)
6:45 AM (MST) 5:45 AM (PST)

KingdomKeysWithCassandraMack.com

The Soul Fast Workbook. Copyright © 2017 by Cassandra Mack.

About the Author... Cassandra Mack

Cassandra Mack, MSW comes to you with over 17 year of successful experience helping individuals and organizations build capacity, develop potential in people and maximize success. Cassandra has always felt a calling to help others. She is passionate about teaching and coaching people on how to reach their goals, achieve better wellbeing and live out their vision of success. Cassandra is an author, empowerment strategist, ordained minister, life coach, a trained social worker, and a master facilitator who masterfully bridges the clinical and practical with the biblical. Cassandra is also the founder of, *Kingdom Keys With Cassandra Mack Ministries,* which is a dynamic life skills ministry that equips individuals with Bible-based principles for empowered living and whole-life success. For more information about Cassandra Mack's ministry go to: **www.KingdomKeysWithCassandraMack.com**

Cassandra is the CVO of *Strategies for Empowered Living Inc.*, a training and development company that she established in NYC in 2000 that provides professional development training, technical assistance and consulting to health and human service organizations in the following areas: leadership development, management and supervisory skills, interpersonal relationships, youth development and self-care and personal wellbeing in the workplace. For more information about her on-site workplace training and consulting go to: **www.StrategiesForEmpoweredLiving.com**

Cassandra Mack speaks at churches, corporations, clubs, and national conferences. She has written more than ten books that are widely utilized in the human services.

Cassandra Mack is the voice of counsel to thousands around the world through her books, Facebook Pages, YouTube videos and coaching programs. Cassandra has received many awards for her work including the: National Association on Drug Abuse Problems Service Award, The New York City Housing Authority Community Programming Award, the Neighborhood Prevention Network Community Service Award and the Hunter College Alumni Association Emerging Leaders Award. Cassandra holds a Master's Degree in Social Work from the Hunter College School of Social work and a Bachelor of Arts Degree from Brooklyn College.

About Kingdom Keys With Cassandra Mack Ministries

For many people of faith, there's often a disconnect between what is learned in the Bible and how to practically apply this essential wisdom and revelation to our daily lives, our goals and our challenges. At *Kingdom Keys With Cassandra Mack Ministries,* our aim is to help bridge the gap between biblical learning and real life application through Cassandra Mack's innovative teaching style of Kingdom-centered life principles that are found in the Bible.

The reality of life is, each of us is doing the best that we can to figure out how to navigate this life and do so with success and grace. And as we journey towards solutions to the things that challenge us, frustrate us, force us to grow and test our resolve; we need principles that are universal, practical, relevant to our daily lives, rooted in the truth of God's word and that stand the test of time. That's where *Kingdom Keys With Cassandra Mack Ministries* comes in. Cassandra Mack's goal with this ministry is to inspire and equip people with Kingdom-based empowerment strategies to maximize their lives, unlock potential, pursue their goals with confidence and shed the things that are stealing their joy and sabotaging their success. *Kingdom Keys With Cassandra Mack Ministries,* is all about empowering people to operate at maximum capacity by giving them biblical tools to:

1.) Unlock more of their potential
2.) Take targeted steps towards their success
3.) Focus on purpose
4.) Shut the door on stress, mess and drama
5.) Navigate their lives from a place of faith and grace

Why Kingdom Keys With Cassandra Mack Ministries?
Although we firmly believe that connecting with the right bible-based church is paramount to one's spiritual growth and Christian fellowship. There are so many people who may not have a church home or who are homebound or who are seeking but are on the fence between skepticism and faith; and our prayer calls, teachings and online community enables individuals to grow in their faith at their own pace, learn timeless strategies for empowered living, enhance their wellbeing and live their lives from a place of grace. Through our various prayer & teaching calls, inspiring videos, teaching resources as well as consulting, coaching, conferences, retreats, seminars, and leadership development activities primarily led by Cassandra Mack, we are fulfilling our kingdom purpose. For more information go to our ministry website: **KingdomKeysWithCassandraMack.com**

The Soul Fast Workbook. Copyright © 2017 by Cassandra Mack.
P. 6

Table of Contents

Introduction

"Be In Good Health, Even As Your Soul Prospers"
3 John 1:2

Everything that we take in mentally, emotionally and spiritually has a profound effect on our happiness and success. From the things that we see on television and social media, to the conversations we entertain, the pain that we've been through, the resentment that we hold on to, as well as the thoughts that run rampant in our minds throughout the course of the day. You may not realize it, but when your mind is overwrought with negative thoughts and counterproductive self-talk or you're weighed down in your spirit with toxic emotional baggage, it's difficult to feel successful and fully enjoy your life. This is why, it is extremely vital that every now and then, that you do a Master Cleanse for your heart and mind.

Welcome to, *The Soul Fast Workbook*. Throughout these pages, you will embark on your very own personal journey into the care and wellbeing of your soul. You will be equipped with powerful tools and information that will empower you to renew your mind, refresh your spirit and detox from all of the negativity and madness that seeks to eat away at your peace of mind and happiness. Grounded in Biblical principles, *The Soul Fast Workbook* is part journal, part workbook and part self-reflection diary that provides you with food for thought and a writing space so that you can soul search on paper. This way you can observe and self-evaluate your own beliefs, mindsets, emotions and choices as you begin to do the work of preparing your heart and mind to be in good health and prosper.

The Soul Fast Workbook is divided into 4 sections: your thought life, your emotional life, your choices and your relationships. <u>Section 1</u> of *The Soul Fast Workbook,* focuses on *The Mind*. It encompasses day 1 through 10, where you'll be fasting from toxic mindsets and counterproductive self-talk. <u>Section 2</u> focuses on *The Heart*. It encompasses days 11 through 20, where you'll be detoxing from emotions that bring down your mood and intensify fear-based feelings like: inadequacy, self-loathing, rejection, dejection, and envy. <u>Section 3</u> deals with *The Will*. It includes day 21 through 30 where you'll be assessing your choices so that you can figure out how to stop making decisions that work against your own wellbeing and success. <u>Section 4</u> focuses on your *Relationships*. It encompasses day 31 through 40 where you'll be evaluating your relationships so that you clearly determine which relationships are producing good fruit in your life and which ones are draining you and pulling you away from purpose.

If you've never done a Soul Fast before, let me tell you what it is. A *Soul Fast,* unlike a fast from edible food or from a particular activity like television or social media is a type of master cleanse for your soul where you abstain from the unhealthy mental junk foods that we tend to feed our hearts and minds like: self-doubt, self-loathing, inadequacy, worry, bitterness, despair, envy and fear. When we chew and stew on negative thoughts and emotions, we are actually feeding on toxins that are poisonous to the wellbeing of our souls. Over time, this negative energy that we are carrying on the

The Soul Fast Workbook. Copyright © 2017 by Cassandra Mack.

inside affects our happiness, health, productivity, relationships and it moves us away from living our most enriched and powerful life.

You were divinely designed to live a fruitful life and enjoy the benefits of healthy wellbeing. When all is well with your soul, you are empowered to live authentically, resiliently and victoriously. In fact, the Bible stresses the importance of a prosperous soul ...one that is well, whole, peaceful, anxious for nothing and joyful. Here's the scripture for it: **3 John 1:2** *"Beloved, I wish above all things that you may prosper and be in health, even as your soul prospers."* This scripture lets us know that we were divinely designed to experience prosperity not just physically; but spiritually and psychologically too. However, it can be hard as heck to feel like you are winning, if your heart is saturated with resentment, envy, ingratitude and self-pity and if your mind is consumed with a never-ending laundry list of all the things in life that annoy you, offend you and hurt you. Toxic thoughts come into our minds to steal, kill and destroy our hopes and dreams, in order to defeat us in the spirit so that we abort our purpose and forfeit our destiny. *Enough already!* This negative thinking has got to stop if you are to enjoy your life to the fullest and leave some sort of legacy that lets the world know that you made a difference to the Kingdom in your own unique way. But none of this can happen unless you do the inner work to keep yourself in a good mental and emotional place.

Do you want a soul that is healthy and whole? Then let's start clearing away the clutter together as you work through *The Soul Fast Workbook.*

Perhaps you've never thought about going on a soul fast before or maybe you've done one before and you already know how beneficial it is. Whether you've done a soul fast in the past or if this is your first time, I want you to know this: *A soul fast is just as vital to your personal productivity and wellbeing as fasting from edible junk food.* While most people view fasting as a quick way to drop a few pounds, like with *The Master Cleanse Lemonade Diet,* a *Soul Fast* is different. It's about shedding the weight of ...unproductive mindsets, misguided belief systems that bog you down with excess baggage and self-defeating attitudes that make your spirit heavy and eat up your personal power. At its' core, a *Soul Fast* is about being emptied of the unhealthy aspects of self or ego, and becoming filled with more of God's power and wisdom. What's more is, fasting doesn't just eliminate toxins, it brings clarity to the mind, greater revelation to the spirit and deeper breakthroughs for the next season of your life.

The reality of life is this: Everyone *and I do mean Everyone* ...needs a breakthrough at some point in their lives – be it: a breakthrough answer to a problem that's been weighing heavily on their mind, a breakthrough idea for your business, a breakthrough strategy for your ministry, a breakthrough in your finances, a breakthrough of a new measure of grace to deal with a difficult situation, a breakthrough in your health or a breakthrough in your perspective about a challenging situation that you cannot change. Spiritual fasting brings forth breakthrough, because fasting and prayer break the yoke of mental strongholds and spiritual bondage. Plus, it brings about a deeper release of God's presence, power, and provision. The Bible affirms this notion in the following scripture <u>Isaiah 58:6</u> *"Is not this the kind of fasting I have chosen: to loose the chains of injustice and untie the cords of the yoke, to set the oppressed free and break every yoke?*

With that being said: *Why Should You Go On A Soul Fast?* Here's why: A lot of us go to great lengths to beautify and care for the outside, but we don't always put that

The Soul Fast Workbook. Copyright © 2017 by Cassandra Mack.

same energy and attention into the care and feeding of our souls. And, in order to operate at maximum capacity, physically, spiritually and psychologically, we have to become just as intentional about what we put into our hearts and minds as we do our bodies. Manicures and pedicures are nice self-pampering treats, but at the same time we cannot forget to beautify and purify our souls.

As humans, we are tri-part beings (body, soul and spirit). We live in a *body*, we possess a *soul* and at the core we are *spirit*. The <u>*body*</u> is the physical house or corporeal dwelling place that houses our soul and spirit and enables us to engage and interact with the material world physically. The <u>*spirit*</u> is the non-material part of our existence that was made in God's image and likeness. It's the awareness element in humanity that discerns and knows truth and enables us to have an intimate relationship with God. The <u>*spirit*</u> is the aspect of our being that is interconnected with God, just like a single unseen cell in the human body is interconnected to all the other cells that belong to that human body. The soul and the spirit are connected, but distinguishable from one another as noted in <u>Hebrews 4: 12.</u> The <u>*soul*</u> is the essence of our psychological make-up and how we perceive reality; it is who we are individually through our personality, perspective and temperament. The <u>*soul*</u> is the seat of our individuality and distinctiveness. Now the *soul* has three parts to it as well. The soul is comprised of our mind, emotions and our will. While our <u>*bodies*</u> enable us to physically interact with the material world through our 5 physical senses; our *souls* enable us to engage the world mentally and emotionally through our thoughts, feelings, motives, and desires.

Every desire you have, every goal you hope to achieve, every dream you envision yourself fulfilling, every idea, feeling and belief you have; all emanate from your *soul*. Therefore, if your soul is weighed down with negativity, you cannot fully enjoy your life and show up for life as your best, brightest and most authentic self. Hence the scripture in <u>Proverbs 23:7:</u> "As a man thinketh in his heart, so is he." So, the question for you to ponder as you go through *The Soul Fast Workbook,* is this: *Who do you think you are in your heart of hearts, when it's just YOU and YOUR THOUGHTS? Because whoever* **THAT PERSON** *is ...that's how you will show up for life and personally experience each and every day of your existence on earth.*

When your soul is whole, your mind is clearer and more productive, your spirit is more discerning and attuned to the things of God and you experience greater success and personal effectiveness in every area of your life.

A Soul Fast Is Not About What You're Eating
It's All About ... What's Eating You?

Have you ever noticed that when you're emotionally overloaded and mentally stressed that it's difficult to stay focused and even the simplest of life's pleasures seem harder to enjoy? Reason being is when our souls are congested with toxic thoughts and emotional

> **"We work to feed our appetites. Meanwhile our souls go hungry"**
> **Ecclesiastes 6:7.**

baggage from the past, or even the present for that matter, it affects our ability to enjoy our lives and maximize our true potential. When we let our minds continually stew on negative incidents, or when we keep feeding into the dysfunctional dynamics of a draining relationship or when we keep investing our time and energy in people who do not value, respect or treat us kindly, or if our behavior is self-absorbed and drama-driven; we don't live life to the fullest because we are not living from our most powerful place of inner wisdom and healthy wellbeing. This is why it's vital, to not just detox our bodies from all of the unhealthy junk that we eat, but more importantly to detox our souls from the negative junk that we feed into as well as the toxic self-talk and discouraging beliefs that we feed our hearts and minds.

There Are Some Breakthroughs That Only Come Through Prayer & Fasting

There's a story in, _Matthew 17: 14-21_, where a father has a son who needed healing and deliverance; so, he brings him to Jesus. The father goes on to tell Jesus that his son was suffering greatly. In fact, this man tried going to the disciples first, but they were unable to heal his son. In the end, Jesus heals the boy. Afterwards the disciples ask Jesus why they weren't able to bring the boy to a place of healing. Here was Jesus' response, _Matthew 17: 20-21_ ... _"So, Jesus said to them, "Because of your unbelief; for assuredly, I say to you, if you have faith as a mustard seed, you will say to this mountain, 'Move from here to there,' and it will move; and nothing will be impossible for you. However, this kind does not go out except by prayer and fasting."_

Often when we hear this story, we focus solely on verse 20 while not fully appreciating the significance of verse 21, but verse 21 is the key that unlocks the essential wisdom needed for total victory ..._21"However, this <u>kind</u> does not go out except by prayer and fasting."_

The Soul Fast Workbook. Copyright © 2017 by Cassandra Mack.

While your *"**kind**"* of thing, need, situation, or issue may not be as severe as the boy in this story, the takeaway is this: *There are some answers and breakthroughs that can only come to us by way of prayer and fasting.*

What **kind** of *thing, need, issue, emotional wound* or *situation* in your life can only be resolved, healed or understood by way of prayer and fasting? Take a moment to think about it. Then, write down what comes to mind and reflect on it.

_____

_____

_____

_____

_____

_____

_____

_____

_____

_____

_____

_____

_____

_____

_____

_____

_____

_____

_____

_____

Identify Your Reasons & Set Your Goal

What Are Your Reasons for Going On This Fast?

Maybe you, like me, want the rest of your year to be better and more fulfilling than last year or the year before. Perhaps you want more from your life than you are currently experiencing and more of God's presence, power and provision. Whether it's more peace, more joy, more confidence, more healing, more comfort, more connection, more direction, more provision, more purpose, more clarity ...or a very specific goal in a particular area of your life; take a few moments to *search all the inner depths of your heart* so you can identify the reason or reasons why you are going on this soul fast.

> "The spirit of man is the lamp of the LORD, searching all the inner depths of the heart."
> Proverbs 20:27

As you commit by faith to sit in the presence of God by way of prayer and fasting, know that He will direct your path *Proverbs 3:6* and answer your prayers *Psalm 34:17.* So pray expectantly and know that God always answers prayers. It's up to us to discern if the answer is: *Yes, No* or *Not Yet.* And whatever you do, don't worry about how you will complete the soul fast. Just make the commitment to do it and take it one day at a time. You can do this! Believe by faith that you can do all things through Christ who strengthens you *Philippians 4:13.* **Repeat:** *I believe by faith that I can do this soul fast.*

In the space below, write down your reason or reasons for going on this soul fast. Let your reason serve as motivation to stick with it.

The reason I am going on this soul fast is because...

_____

_____

_____

_____

_____

_____

_____

_____

_____

_____

_____

_____

_____

_____

_____

_____

◎**Now turn your reason into a goal that you wish to accomplish by going on this soul fast.**

The goal(s) that I intend to accomplish for myself by way of my soul fast is...

_____

_____

_____

_____

_____

_____

_____

_____

_____

_____

_____

_____

_____

_____

_____

_____

_____

_____

Suggested Steps to Help You Stick With Your Soul Fast

1. **Set Your Alarm For 30 Minutes Earlier.** You should set aside at least 30 minutes each morning to pray and complete the daily worksheets in this workbook. And remember *Prayer* is simply talking to God. Prayer can be out loud or in your head, private or public, formal or informal. You can pray sitting, standing, kneeling or lying down. You can pray to God about whatever is on your mind. You can talk to God about your plans for the day, your plans for your life, your hopes, desires and dreams, the areas in your life that you want to improve, the areas in your life where you feel insecure, afraid, hurt or angry. You can pray for wisdom, guidance and direction. You can talk to God about your needs and worries and cast your cares on the Lord. You can pray for the mental and emotional strength to deal with a specific situation or the courage and confidence to make a hard decision. There is no topic that is off limits when it comes to talking to God. God loves you. God created you to have a relationship with Him. And God has a purpose and a plan for your life; so, it just makes sense to be in daily communication with The One who knows what's best for you and who knows what you need before you even ask.

2. **Gather Your Materials.** (Bring your Bible, a pen, a composition notebook and your Soul Fast Workbook) (If you don't have a physical Bible you can read the Bible online at: www.biblegateway.com or www.bible.com

3. **Create An Atmosphere For Answers.** *What is an atmosphere for answers?* It's a quiet space where you can go to pray, mediate, clear your head, read your Bible and complete the *Soul Fast Workbook* assignment for the day without being disturbed.

4. **Take It One Day At A Time.** There are 40 worksheets in this workbook, one worksheet for each day of the soul fast. Focus on one day at a time. You can do this!

5. **Invite A Friend To Join You On Your Soul Fast or Tell Your Church or Women's Group About The Soul Fast.** We were not created to walk alone. We were created for fellowship, connection and community. The benefit of doing the soul fast with a friend is: you will have an accountability partner, you can pray for one another, encourage each other and inspire each other to stay the course. Don't forget to tell your friend or group to get their own copies of the workbook; since distributing the workbook without the author's expressed permission is a form of robbery and all things should be done in decency and order. If you have a friend who wants to participate in the soul fast but is unable to purchase the *Soul Fast Workbook,* why not be a blessing to this ministry and your friend by purchasing the workbook for your friend if he or she is not able to purchase their own copy at this time.

6. **Select A Gospel Song You Love and Make It Your Soul Fast Theme Song.** Gospel music can speak to your soul in ways that words cannot express. When you cannot find the words to say, gospel music can minister to your soul right where you are. This is why you will be selecting a gospel song that ministers to your spirit and you're going to make it your theme song for the soul fast. Wake up to your personal theme song. Embody the message of your theme song. Play your theme song before you start each day of the fast. You can even make it your ringtone. Believe it or not: having a gospel song as your soul fast theme song will set your mind on what you can accomplish through Christ who strengthens you. It will inspire you to keep on pressing on, on the hard days. Some of my personal favorites are: *"Go Get It" by: Mary, Mary, "Open My Heart by Yolanda Adams" "The Best In Me" by Marvin Sapp, "Stand" by Donnie McClurkin, "Imagine Me" by Kirk Franklin, "Never Give Up" by Yolanda Adams, "No Weapon" by Fred Hammond "I Need You Now" Smokey Norful, "Alabaster Box by CeCe Winans and "Nobody Knows Me Better" by Vicki Yohe.* Whatever Gospel song you elect to use as your personal theme song for this soul fast, let it minister to your spirit each day of this fast.

7. **Fast From Eating One Food Item While You Are On The Soul Fast.** It can be anything from chocolate to cake to coffee to red meat. As I mentioned previously, the purpose of a soul fast is to abstain from the toxic things we feed our hearts and minds. However, by giving up one edible thing that goes into our mouths, we deny the flesh and prepare our hearts and minds for the spiritual shift that's about to happen in our lives. By fasting from one food item that's a real sacrifice for you, you train your mind and emotions to align with your spirit rather than work against it. When the mind and body are working together in harmony, we develop the spiritual fruit of self-control. But always consult with your doctor before going on any type of food item fast and make sure to get the okay from your primary care physician.

8. **Fast From Drinking Alcohol While On The Soul Fast**. You want to keep a clear head as you do the work of this soul fast. Have you ever had one too many and it affected your mood and attitude or how you felt physically? Since alcohol also known as spirits can affect your mood, impair your judgment and lower your inhibitions it can also adversely affect your decision making and cause you to be receptive to things that you normally wouldn't be receptive to when your mind is sober. During this fast, you want to keep your spirit as clear and clean as possible so that you can be more receptive to the leading and prompting of the Holy Spirit.

9. **Join our Facebook Community.** Make sure to become part of our Kingdom Keys Community on Facebook. Facebook.com/groups/kingdomkeyswithcassandramack

10. **Sign Up for Updates by Email**. www.KingdomKeysWithCassandraMack.com

Section 1
The Mind

Fasting From Toxic Thinking

The Soul Fast Workbook. Copyright © 2017 by Cassandra Mack.

The Mind: Fasting From Toxic Thinking

"Take Every Thought Captive" 2 Corinthians 10:5

In this section of your *Soul Fast Workbook,* you will be taking 10 days to fast from toxic thinking. You will pay close attention to the kinds of thoughts that you tend to think about a lot, ruminate over and dwell on, so that you can become more aware of how your thought life is affecting your focus, progress, happiness and wellbeing. This way, you can begin to take your thoughts captive and reject the negative ones that come into your mind to pull you in the direction of negativity, or to make you mentally re-live a past event that you put behind you, to prick at old wounds that are in the process of healing and that try to exalt themselves against what you know to be true about God's word (The Bible) and your identity as a child of God (Who the Bible says you are).

Did you know that without even thinking about it, we talk to ourselves all day every day? And for most of us, this self-talk is negative and discouraging. What's more is this internal conversation that runs rampant through our mind eventually becomes part of our core belief system, which frames our outlook, identity, conduct and habits. If our outlook is self-defeating, then everything that flows out of this outlook will be rooted in self-defeat and inadequacy. This is why we need to affirm our authentic identity by reminding ourselves that we were *Fearfully* and *Wonderfully* made. In fact, before you were fully formed, when you were just a blip on the pediatrician's sonogram screen, you were magnificence in motion and God knew you by name. This is why the bible reminds us in <u>Jeremiah 1:5</u> of this very important piece of information.... *"Before I formed you in the womb I knew you, before you were born I set you apart."* We were all created in magnificence and brilliance. So, if you were created in magnificence and brilliance then it goes without saying that you already have greatness inside of you ...all you have to do is nurture your seeds of greatness by shifting the way you think and see yourself and by aligning your beliefs with the word of God. In this section of *The Soul Fast Workbook* you will learn how to take your thoughts captive <u>2 Corinthians 10:5</u> and renew your mind <u>Romans 12:2</u>. This will create a paradigm shift in the way you think, feel, respond to situations and circumstances and it will revolutionize the way you live.

<u>Here Are Just A Few Examples of Commonly Held Negative Beliefs That You May Need To Detox From During This Soul Fast</u>

1. My best days are behind me.
2. Everyone hates me.
3. I'll never get a good job.
4. I will never get married.
5. I won't be successful.
6. I will be broke all my life.
7. My life will never get better.
8. I am ugly.
9. I am worthless.

It's important to keep in mind that negative beliefs are just that ..." *beliefs*" they are not truth or facts. Therefore, as you take the next 10 days to examine your thought life, you will be replacing all of the toxic lies that you've been led to believe with the truth of God's word. On the following page, I have provided some bible scriptures that you can say and pray in order to replace negative mindsets and faulty beliefs. Or you can feel free to search for your own bible verses. Let's begin.

The Soul Fast Workbook. Copyright © 2017 by Cassandra Mack.

Here Are Some Selected Bible Scriptures
That You Can Feast On As You Fast From Toxic Thinking

Ephesians 4: 29 Do not let any unwholesome talk come out of your mouths, but only what is helpful for building others up according to their needs, that it may benefit those who listen.

Romans 12: 2 And be not conformed to this world: but be transformed by the renewing of your mind, that you may prove what is that good, and acceptable, and perfect, will of God.

Philippians 4:8 Finally, brethren, whatever things are true, whatever things are noble, whatever things are just, whatever things are pure, whatever things are lovely, whatever things are of good report, if there is any virtue and if there is anything praiseworthy-- meditate on these things.

2 Corinthians 10:5 Casting down arguments and every high thing that exalts itself against the knowledge of God, bringing every thought into captivity to the obedience of Christ,

Ephesians 4: 23-24 to be made new in the attitude of your minds; and to put on the new self, created to be like God in true righteousness and holiness.

Philippians 4: 13 I can do all things through Christ which strengthens me.

Deuteronomy 28:6 You will be blessed when you come in and blessed when you go out.

Romans 8:37 Yet in all these things we are more than conquerors through Him who loved us."

Psalm 139:14 I will praise you; for I am fearfully and wonderfully made: marvelous are your works; and that my soul knows right well.

Colossians 3: 16. Let the word of Christ dwell in you richly in all wisdom, teaching and admonishing one another in psalms and hymns and spiritual songs, singing with grace in your hearts to the Lord.

Ephesians 6: 14-18 Stand therefore, having girded your waist with truth, having put on the breastplate of righteousness, 15 and having shod your feet with the preparation of the gospel of peace; 16 above all, taking the shield of faith with which you will be able to quench all the fiery darts of the wicked one. 17 And take the helmet of salvation, and the sword of the Spirit, which is the word of God; 18 praying always with all prayer and supplication in the Spirit, being watchful to this end with all perseverance and supplication for all the saints.

The Soul Fast Workbook. Copyright © 2017 by Cassandra Mack.

Day 1

❋Today's Date: _____

Worksheet for Day 1

Fasting From Self-Defeating Thinking

1. **Pray:** Start your day with prayer. Thank God for all of your blessings including the blessing to be able to wake up and see a brand-new day today. Give God the praise by telling God how great He is. Talk to God about whatever is on your heart this morning. Ask God to reveal any mindsets, beliefs or outlooks that you need to reject and "fast" from because they are either: holding you back, undermining your success or they're not in alignment with who the Bible says you are as a child of God.

2. **Identify The Self-Defeating Thought That You Intend To Reject Today:**
   _____
   _____
   _____

3. **Reject It:**
   Say: **I Reject** …. _____
   (fill in the blank with the thought/belief/mindset that you intend to reject).

4. **Renew Your Mind By Replacing The Self-Defeating Thought With One of The Selected Scriptures Or You Can Use Another Bible Verse:**
   ♥ *I Am Replacing The Thought With This Bible Scripture:*
   _____
   _____
   _____
   _____
   _____
   _____
   _____

5. **Meditate On Your Selected Scripture and Think About What God Is Saying To You Personally By Way Of This Scripture:**

6. **Declare:** *I am* (say your name) and then say your bible scripture out loud.

7. **Journal Space …** ✍
Following is your journal space. You can write down your thoughts, feelings, insights, prayers or anything else that you feel led to write. You can also write down any questions that you want to explore during your quiet time with God.

Day 2

✹Today's Date: ______________________

Worksheet for Day 2

Fasting From Self-Defeating Thinking

1. **Pray:** Start your day with prayer. Thank God for all of your blessings including the blessing to be able to wake up and see a brand-new day today. Give God the praise by telling God how great He is. Talk to God about whatever is on your heart this morning. Ask God to reveal any mindsets, beliefs or outlooks that you need to reject and "fast" from because they are either: holding you back, undermining your success or they're not in alignment with who the Bible says you are as a child of God.

2. **Identify The Self-Defeating Thought That You Intend To Reject Today:**

____

____

____

3. **Reject It**.
   Say: **I Reject** .... ______________________________
   (fill in the blank with the thought/belief/mindset that you intend to reject).

4. **Renew Your Mind By Replacing The Self-Defeating Thought With One of The Selected Scriptures Or You Can Use Another Bible Verse:**

♥ *I Am Replacing The Thought With This Bible Scripture:*

____

____

____

____

____

____

____

5. **Meditate On Your Selected Scripture and Think About What God Is Saying To You Personally By Way Of This Scripture:**

6. **Declare:** *I am (*say your name*)* and then say your bible scripture out loud.

7. **Journal Space ...** ✍

Following is your journal space. You can write down your thoughts, feelings, insights, prayers or anything else that you feel led to write. You can also write down any questions that you want to explore during your quiet time with God.

Day 3

Worksheet for Day 3

Fasting From Self-Defeating Thinking

1. **Pray:** Start your day with prayer. Thank God for all of your blessings including the blessing to be able to wake up and see a brand-new day today. Give God the praise by telling God how great He is. Talk to God about whatever is on your heart this morning. Ask God to reveal any mindsets, beliefs or outlooks that you need to reject and "fast" from because they are either: holding you back, undermining your success or they're not in alignment with who the Bible says you are as a child of God.

2. **Identify The Self-Defeating Thought That You Intend To Reject Today:**
   _____
   _____
   _____

3. **Reject It:**
   Say: **I Reject** …. _____
   (fill in the blank with the thought/belief/mindset that you intend to reject).

4. **Renew Your Mind By Replacing The Self-Defeating Thought With One of The Selected Scriptures Or You Can Use Another Bible Verse:**
   ♥ *I Am Replacing The Thought With This Bible Scripture:*
   _____
   _____
   _____
   _____
   _____
   _____
   _____

5. **Meditate On Your Selected Scripture and Think About What God Is Saying To You Personally By Way Of This Scripture:**

6. **Declare:** *I am* (say your name) and then say your bible scripture out loud.

7. **Journal Space …** ✍
Following is your journal space. You can write down your thoughts, feelings, insights, prayers or anything else that you feel led to write. You can also write down any questions that you want to explore during your quiet time with God.

The Soul Fast Workbook. Copyright © 2017 by Cassandra Mack.

Day 4

❋Today's Date: _____

Worksheet for Day 4

Fasting From Self-Defeating Thinking

1. **Pray:** Start your day with prayer. Thank God for all of your blessings including the blessing to be able to wake up and see a brand-new day today. Give God the praise by telling God how great He is. Talk to God about whatever is on your heart this morning. Ask God to reveal any mindsets, beliefs or outlooks that you need to reject and "fast" from because they are either: holding you back, undermining your success or they're not in alignment with who the Bible says you are as a child of God.

2. **Identify The Self-Defeating Thought That You Intend To Reject Today:**
   _____
   _____
   _____

3. **Reject It:**
   Say: **I Reject** …. _____
   (fill in the blank with the thought/belief/mindset that you intend to reject).

4. **Renew Your Mind By Replacing The Self-Defeating Thought With One of The Selected Scriptures Or You Can Use Another Bible Verse:**
   ♥ *I Am Replacing The Thought With This Bible Scripture:*
   _____
   _____
   _____
   _____
   _____
   _____
   _____

5. **Meditate On Your Selected Scripture and Think About What God Is Saying To You Personally By Way Of This Scripture:**

6. **Declare:** *I am* (say your name) and then say your bible scripture out loud.

7. **Journal Space … ✍**
Following is your journal space. You can write down your thoughts, feelings, insights, prayers or anything else that you feel led to write. You can also write down any questions that you want to explore during your quiet time with God.

The Soul Fast Workbook. Copyright © 2017 by Cassandra Mack.

Day 5

❋Today's Date: _____

Worksheet for Day 5

Fasting From Self-Defeating Thinking

1. **Pray:** Start your day with prayer. Thank God for all of your blessings including the blessing to be able to wake up and see a brand-new day today. Give God the praise by telling God how great He is. Talk to God about whatever is on your heart this morning. Ask God to reveal any mindsets, beliefs or outlooks that you need to reject and "fast" from because they are either: holding you back, undermining your success or they're not in alignment with who the Bible says you are as a child of God.

2. **Identify The Self-Defeating Thought That You Intend To Reject Today:**
_____
_____
_____

3. **Reject It:**
Say: **I Reject** …. _____
(fill in the blank with the thought/belief/mindset that you intend to reject).

4. **Renew Your Mind By Replacing The Self-Defeating Thought With One of The Selected Scriptures Or You Can Use Another Bible Verse:**
♥ *I Am Replacing The Thought With This Bible Scripture:*
_____
_____
_____
_____
_____
_____
_____

5. **Meditate On Your Selected Scripture and Think About What God Is Saying To You Personally By Way Of This Scripture:**

6. **Declare:** *I am* (say your name) and then say your bible scripture out loud.

7. **Journal Space …** ✍
Following is your journal space. You can write down your thoughts, feelings, insights, prayers or anything else that you feel led to write. You can also write down any questions that you want to explore during your quiet time with God.

The Soul Fast Workbook. Copyright © 2017 by Cassandra Mack.

The Importance of Knowing Who You Are

The most powerful affirmation in the world is the statement, **I AM** because whatever follows your, **I AM** is a verbal declaration of who you believe you are as well as what you are calling into your life.

Never forget that the word "**AM**" is a verb and a verb is an action word, so we need to be mindful of the kind of action that we are calling into our lives whenever we say the words ...I AM. In fact, if you think back to elementary school and recall the lessons on conjugating verbs, you'll remember that the verb "**AM**" is the first-person singular present tense of the verb "To BE" which means (to exist). ...So, whatever comes after your, *I AM* you are essentially giving it permission to exist in your life. When we say things like I am so stupid; we give the spirit of inadequacy permission to enter into our thought life and impact our self-esteem.

This is why it's crucial that we speak life into ourselves by declaring the word of God over our lives. We have the power to call our FEARFULNESS into existence with the declaration I AM FEARFULLY MADE. We have the authority to call our WONDERFULNESS into existence with the declaration I AM WONDERFULLY made. We have the power to call our MARVELOUSNESS into existence with the declaration I AM Marvelous ...and since Marvelous are Thy works and I AM included in God's marvelous works, then this means that I AM marvelous too. This way when self-defeating thoughts try to fill your head with lies, you can replace each and every lie with The TRUTH of GOD'S WORD.

The reason so many of us ...including Believers; have such a hard time winning the battle in our minds and overcoming counterproductive thinking is because we're constantly being bombarded with negativity. For many of us, most of our lives we've been psychologically saturated with put downs and criticism. And over time, these negative words take root in our thought life (like small seeds or weeds that choke the life out of our good fruit) and this causes us to focus on the ~~I Am Nots,~~ such as: *I am not capable* or *I am not good enough* or *I am not smart*. But God wants to show us our **I Am**, such as: "*I am more than a conqueror,*" (Romans 8:37) and "*I am blessed coming in and blessed going out,*" (Deuteronomy 28:6) and "*I am fearfully and wonderfully made.*" (Psalm 139:14)

Where do negative thoughts come from? They come from the words that are spoken into our lives by others as well as the words that we say to ourselves via our internal dialogue that flows through our minds throughout the course of our day. Perhaps when you were a kid, a parent or teacher was extremely critical of you and you thought to yourself, "*I am not that smart.*" Or maybe you didn't make the football team or cheerleading squad so your mind told you ..."*I am not talented.*" Or perhaps you were rejected and criticized so your mind told you "*I am not good enough.*" Or you look in the mirror and compare yourself to other people and tell yourself, "*I am not beautiful.*"

When we accept self-defeating beliefs as self-evident truths they create yokes and mental strongholds that are hard to break. And this poisons your mind with lies that hold you back from grabbing hold of all of the success, joy, peace and prosperity that's yours for the taking.

This is why it's important to remind yourself often that ...If you were created in the image and likeness of THE GREAT I AM THAT I AM, and He breathed his breath of life spirit in you at creation so that you could become a living soul (Genesis 2:7) then greatness is the higher reality of who YOU ARE...and anything contrary to that is the LIE. God was so intent on making sure that we understood the level of potency of the power that flows through us, holds us up, empowers us and gives us grace ....that when it was time for Moses to carry out his assignment to tell Pharaoh to ...let my people go; and Moses was apprehensive about it, Exodus 3:14 lets us know this ...."*And God said unto Moses, I AM THAT I AM: and He said, Thus shalt thou say unto the children of Israel, I AM hath sent me unto you.*"

So, whenever we are tempted to give in to self-defeatist thinking, God's statement to Moses is a statement for us all. And it's to serve notice that the same *I AM THAT I AM* that was with Moses during that time in Bible history is the same *I AM THAT I AM* who is with you and me today. So, know that you are not alone, The Great I AM is with you every step of the way.

Do you remember the story of, *Green Eggs and Ham*, by Dr. Seuss? This was one of my favorite childhood stories because it reinforced the importance of knowing who you are, even when other people reject what you have to offer. It was clear from the first sentence in *Green Eggs and Ham* that *Sam-I-Am* knew who he was and he was not going to be defeated by negativity or deterred by rejection. In fact, the character *Sam-I-Am* was so relentless with respect to his purpose (to get the Grouch to open up his mind and try something new) that he affirmed his identity throughout the entire story by repeatedly stating "*I-Am-Sam*" "*Sam-I-Am.*" I don't believe that it's an accident that in the children's book, *Green Eggs and Ham,* the story opens up with Sam stating for himself who he was, with the Bold Declaration ...*I-Am-Sam.* Not only did *Sam-I-Am* start the conversation by DECLARING WHO HE WAS .... *I-Am-Sam*, but in case there was any confusion about his identity, he re-introduced himself by confirming his identity with the declaration... *Sam-I-Am.* In life, you've got to know who you are. As Believers, we have to know who we are in Christ. Never let anyone define who you are or make you believe that WHO you are, is not enough. And in case other people want to define you by your past, your social status, your struggles or anything else that does not align with the reality of who God says that you are in the Bible, do like *Sam-I-Am* and be relentless about defining yourself for yourself. In the end, people can criticize you, call you names, reject you and label you, but the only identity that counts is the one that lines up with the word of God. *Who does God say you are?* That's the only description that truly describes the totality of who you are.

Day 6

❋Today's Date: _____

Worksheet for Day 6

Fasting From Self-Defeating Thinking

1. **Pray:** Start your day with prayer. Thank God for all of your blessings including the blessing to be able to wake up and see a brand-new day today. Give God the praise by telling God how great He is. Talk to God about whatever is on your heart this morning. Ask God to reveal any mindsets, beliefs or outlooks that you need to reject and "fast" from because they are either: holding you back, undermining your success or they're not in alignment with who the Bible says you are as a child of God.

2. Identify The Self-Defeating Thought That You Intend To Reject Today:
_____
_____
_____

3. Reject It:
Say: **I Reject** …. _____
(fill in the blank with the thought/belief/mindset that you intend to reject).

4. Renew Your Mind By Replacing The Self-Defeating Thought With One of The Selected Scriptures Or You Can Use Another Bible Verse:
♥ *I Am Replacing The Thought With This Bible Scripture:*
_____
_____
_____
_____
_____
_____

5. Meditate On Your Selected Scripture and Think About What God Is Saying To You Personally By Way Of This Scripture:

6. Declare: *I am* (say your name) and then say your bible scripture out loud.

7. Journal Space … 🖎
Following is your journal space. You can write down your thoughts, feelings, insights, prayers or anything else that you feel led to write. You can also write down any questions that you want to explore during your quiet time with God.

Day 7

✸Today's Date: _____

Worksheet for Day 7

Fasting From Self-Defeating Thinking

1. **Pray:** Start your day with prayer. Thank God for all of your blessings including the blessing to be able to wake up and see a brand-new day today. Give God the praise by telling God how great He is. Talk to God about whatever is on your heart this morning. Ask God to reveal any mindsets, beliefs or outlooks that you need to reject and "fast" from because they are either: holding you back, undermining your success or they're not in alignment with who the Bible says you are as a child of God.

2. **Identify The Self-Defeating Thought That You Intend To Reject Today:**
   _____
   _____
   _____

3. **Reject It:**
   Say: **I Reject** .... _____
   (fill in the blank with the thought/belief/mindset that you intend to reject).

4. **Renew Your Mind By Replacing The Self-Defeating Thought With One of The Selected Scriptures Or You Can Use Another Bible Verse:**
   ♥ *I Am Replacing The Thought With This Bible Scripture:*
   _____
   _____
   _____
   _____
   _____
   _____
   _____

5. **Meditate On Your Selected Scripture and Think About What God Is Saying To You Personally By Way Of This Scripture:**

6. **Declare:** *I am (say your name)* and then say your bible scripture out loud.

7. **Journal Space ...** ✍
Following is your journal space. You can write down your thoughts, feelings, insights, prayers or anything else that you feel led to write. You can also write down any questions that you want to explore during your quiet time with God.

The Soul Fast Workbook. Copyright © 2017 by Cassandra Mack.

The Soul Fast Workbook. Copyright © 2017 by Cassandra Mack.

Day 8

Worksheet for Day 8

Fasting From Self-Defeating Thinking

1. **Pray:** Start your day with prayer. Thank God for all of your blessings including the blessing to be able to wake up and see a brand-new day today. Give God the praise by telling God how great He is. Talk to God about whatever is on your heart this morning. Ask God to reveal any mindsets, beliefs or outlooks that you need to reject and "fast" from because they are either: holding you back, undermining your success or they're not in alignment with who the Bible says you are as a child of God.

2. **Identify The Self-Defeating Thought That You Intend To Reject Today:**
   _____
   _____
   _____

3. **Reject It:**
   Say: **I Reject** …. _____
   _____(fill in the blank with the thought/belief/mindset that you intend to reject)._

4. **Renew Your Mind By Replacing The Self-Defeating Thought With One of The Selected Scriptures Or You Can Use Another Bible Verse:**
   ♥ _I Am Replacing The Thought With This Bible Scripture:_
   _____
   _____
   _____
   _____
   _____
   _____

5. **Meditate On Your Selected Scripture and Think About What God Is Saying To You Personally By Way Of This Scripture:**

6. **Declare:** _I am (say your name)_ and then say your bible scripture out loud.

7. **Journal Space …** ✍
   Following is your journal space. You can write down your thoughts, feelings, insights, prayers or anything else that you feel led to write. You can also write down any questions that you want to explore during your quiet time with God.

Day 9

❋Today's Date: _____

Worksheet for Day 9

Fasting From Self-Defeating Thinking

1. **Pray:** Start your day with prayer. Thank God for all of your blessings including the blessing to be able to wake up and see a brand-new day today. Give God the praise by telling God how great He is. Talk to God about whatever is on your heart this morning. Ask God to reveal any mindsets, beliefs or outlooks that you need to reject and "fast" from because they are either: holding you back, undermining your success or they're not in alignment with who the Bible says you are as a child of God.

2. **Identify The Self-Defeating Thought That You Intend To Reject Today:**

_____
_____
_____

3. **Reject It:**
Say: **I Reject** …. _____
(fill in the blank with the thought/belief/mindset that you intend to reject).

4. **Renew Your Mind By Replacing The Self-Defeating Thought With One of The Selected Scriptures Or You Can Use Another Bible Verse:**
♥ *I Am Replacing The Thought With This Bible Scripture:*

_____
_____
_____
_____
_____
_____

5. **Meditate On Your Selected Scripture and Think About What God Is Saying To You Personally By Way Of This Scripture:**

6. **Declare:** *I am* (say your name) and then say your bible scripture out loud.

7. **Journal Space ...** 🖎
Following is your journal space. You can write down your thoughts, feelings, insights, prayers or anything else that you feel led to write. You can also write down any questions that you want to explore during your quiet time with God.

The Soul Fast Workbook. Copyright © 2017 by Cassandra Mack.

Day 10

❋Today's Date: _____

Worksheet for Day 10

Fasting From Self-Defeating Thinking

1. **Pray:** Start your day with prayer. Thank God for all of your blessings including the blessing to be able to wake up and see a brand-new day today. Give God the praise by telling God how great He is. Talk to God about whatever is on your heart this morning. Ask God to reveal any mindsets, beliefs or outlooks that you need to reject and "fast" from because they are either: holding you back, undermining your success or they're not in alignment with who the Bible says you are as a child of God.

2. **Identify The Self-Defeating Thought That You Intend To Reject Today:**

   _____
   _____
   _____

3. **Reject It:**
   Say: **I Reject** …. _____
   (fill in the blank with the thought/belief/mindset that you intend to reject).

4. **Renew Your Mind By Replacing The Self-Defeating Thought With One of The Selected Scriptures Or You Can Use Another Bible Verse:**

   ♥ *I Am Replacing The Thought With This Bible Scripture:*

   _____
   _____
   _____
   _____
   _____
   _____

5. **Meditate On Your Selected Scripture and Think About What God Is Saying To You Personally By Way Of This Scripture:**

6. **Declare:** *I am* (say your name) and then say your bible scripture out loud.

7. **Journal Space …** 🖎
   Following is your journal space. You can write down your thoughts, feelings, insights, prayers or anything else that you feel led to write. You can also write down any questions that you want to explore during your quiet time with God.

The Soul Fast Workbook. Copyright © 2017 by Cassandra Mack.

Your Check In

✹ Good job!

You made it through the first 10 days of your soul fast. I knew you could do it.

The mere fact that you took 10 days to fast from beliefs and mindsets that are not conducive to your wellbeing is a big accomplishment within itself. Here's why: You've now empowered yourself to transform the quality of your thought life by way of renewing your mind. (Romans 12:2)

1.   Did you fast from toxic beliefs for the entire 10-day period or did you skip a day? Be honest! What was this experience like for you?

2.   Did you compete the worksheets each day? What were you surprised to find yourself writing about?

3.   Did you have any insights, discoveries, revelations or breakthroughs?

4.   What do you believe God is saying to you about your thought life, now that you've taken 10 days to fast from toxic thinking and renew your mind?

5.   Are there any other issues that you consider significant to your mental wellbeing that you feel led to continue working on?

The Soul Fast Workbook. Copyright © 2017 by Cassandra Mack.

The Soul Fast Workbook. Copyright © 2017 by Cassandra Mack.

Section 2
The Heart
Fasting From Toxic Emotions

The Heart: Fasting from Toxic Emotions

"Take no bag for your journey" (Matthew 10:10)

This section of *The Soul Fast Workbook* will deal with your emotional life. For the next 10 days, you will be fasting from toxic emotions that bring you down and keep you in an unhealthy emotional space. Toxic emotions such as: guilt, self-pity, blame, bitterness, anxiety, apathy, self-loathing, envy and resentment eventually become cancerous to your soul and take their toll on your self-esteem, peace of mind and all of your relationships. Just like environmental toxins make us physically sick, toxic emotions entrench themselves in the very fiber of our being making us irrational, emotionally unbalanced and unpleasant to be around. Plus, toxic emotions can cause you to step out of character and behave in ways that are not consistent with the kind of person that you are evolving into and the life you're trying to build. While you may not be able to stop every toxic feeling when it first hits you, you can certainly make a conscious effort not to stay in a negative emotional space and allow a bad mood or embittered feeling to fester to the point where it prevents you from being productive and robs you of days, weeks or even years of your life that you cannot get back.

Now let me be clear: Toxic emotions are not the same thing as having a moment of anger, or indignation or a flash of protective fear that warns you when you're in danger. Toxic emotions are not the same thing as going through the grieving process after a trauma or tragic loss. Toxic emotions are not the same thing as discerning that you cannot trust a particular individual who habitually gossips, slanders others, is envious of you, enjoys seeing others suffer or who comes to you with a hidden agenda. Toxic emotions are not the same thing as getting a bad vibe about a person, because there's something unsettling about them that's not quite right.

In a nutshell, toxic emotions are prolonged and persistent negative feelings that eat away at you mentally and emotionally; robbing you of your joy, peace of mind and your ability to enjoy everyday life and function well. And like a ticking time bomb, if toxic emotions are not managed effectively they can seep into the other areas of your life, causing you to: become unproductive on your job, take your stress and anger out on your kids or spouse, miss out on great opportunities and become the kind of person that even you don't want to be around. And that's when you'll find yourself doing things that undermine your success and progress like: cursing out that annoying coworker or saying something incredibly hurtful to your spouse or binge eating to avoid dealing with yourself, or hitting that bottle of Hennessey as soon as you get home from work, or feeling chronically depressed for no apparent reason, or being irritable all the time to your kids, the dog and the cat. The irony in all of this is that most of us don't even realize when our emotions have taken us to a toxic place, until our anger goes from 0 to

100 or we've sunken so far into depression that we cannot pull ourselves out of it that easily or we've eaten ourselves into three or more dress sizes. This is why it's critical to search your heart regularly through self-reflection, journaling, fasting, meditating on God's word and prayer so that the Holy Spirit can counsel and guide you in order to revealing God's truth for your life. And even though the Holy Spirit does not speak with audible words, The Holy Spirit confirms with God's word. He will bring a particular scripture to mind at just the right time that will serve as your "*Ah Ha*" moment, or someone will say something that resonates with your spirit because it lines up with the timeless truth of God's word. The Holy Spirit guides us through our own conscience and discernment. These are some of the ways how a clean heart is created in us and a right spirit is renewed in us (Psalm 51:10) Going through this process of asking God to create a clean heart in us and renew a right spirit in us, enables us to let go of any toxic emotions that are weighing our spirits down with emotional heaviness, hardening our hearts and preventing us from living a fruitful, resilient and victorious life.

To give you an example of how toxic emotions when allowed to fester can get the best of you, try this exercise: Think about a time when someone did something to you that really pissed you off or hurt you deeply. I'll bet that you can still recall the specific incident like it happened yesterday. I'll also bet that you can bring to mind all of the emotions that you experienced at that time and re-live them mentally, as if it were happening right in this moment even if the incident happened several months or even years ago. *Are you experiencing any of those feelings right now as you recall the incident to mind?* As you remember this unpleasant situation or painful memory have you noticed that your heart is probably beating a little faster and your breathing feels slightly different, or maybe you felt a bit of tension in your lower back or neck or perhaps your mood has changed ...*just a little*, even if it was only for a moment?

What you just experienced was the effect of a toxic emotion. And every time you recall situations like these, you actually re-live all of the emotions all over again in your mind. It doesn't feel good to your soul to re-experience these emotions. *Right*? It's not supposed to feel good to your soul, because our minds are not designed to dwell in toxic spaces, even if that space is in the dwelling place of your own thought life.

Now let's take a minute to release all of the negative feelings that you brought back to mind: *Take a deep breath. Take another. And let's release the negative feeling so that you don't sit with it.* Say the words ...*I release these feelings to God and I am giving this issue to God to carry for me. I give this issue/situation/feeling to God...* Now envision yourself in your mind's eye releasing this feeling to God as if you were giving God a 500-pound bag of bricks with the negative feelings written on each brick. Visualize yourself walking away from the bag of bricks while at the same time feeling lifted in your spirit and emotionally lighter because you are now mindfully aware of God's love and presence, and you are aware that you are no longer carrying this heavy emotional bag. *How do you feel now?* You should feel emotionally lighter. Repeat this exercise as often as you need to, whenever you find yourself feeling overwhelmed emotionally.

Believe it or not, it's easier than you think to develop a spirit of heaviness due to all of the negative emotions that you carry around throughout the day. What's more is when you keep dwelling on the past, you rob yourself of this day that the Lord has made otherwise known as the *Present*. And what happens over time is, this spirit of heaviness takes a toll on your personal wellbeing and self-esteem. Because there is absolutely no way that you can feel good about yourself and happy with your life if you are walking around angry, resentful or depressed most of the time. This is why it's so important to take some well-deserved "me time" for yourself to detox from all of the emotions that are weighing on you so that you can travel through life without the extra emotional weight of excess baggage.

Let's try something. If I were to ask you to make a list of all the emotions you've been feeling lately or that are hard to let go of whenever you see or think about a particular individual or incident: Which emotions would be on your list? Would your list include feelings like: happy, passionate, excited, motivated, serene, peaceful and joyful? Or would your list be more along the lines of: anger, resentment, frustrated, judgmental, scared, confused, worried, fear of being vulnerable, hurt, jealous, insecure, envious and stressed.

Now take this list of emotions and divide it into two side-by-side categories, one category for your positive emotions and the other for the negative emotions, which list is longer? And which list of emotions do you find yourself spending more time dwelling on? It's your life. This means that you are the only one who can change it.

The hard, cold truth about negativity is this: the more we feed on it and allow it to overtake our thoughts and emotions, the more we forfeit our peace of mind and our joy. What happens over time is, your outlook becomes dimmer and the emotional baggage that you're carrying on the inside becomes evident to others. It becomes apparent in your attitude, demeanor, conduct and conversations. You may think that other people don't notice when your vibe is off or your spirit is heavy with anger or if you've got a chip on your shoulder, or that you don't feel as good about yourself as you profess on social media; but they do. Because just like we wear outfits on our bodies that other people can see as soon as we enter a room, we also wear *in-fits* or spiritual energy that other people pick up on as soon as they interact with us ...and sometimes without us even having to say a word. People can feel the weight of whatever you're carrying on the inside because as spirit beings, we always give off a spiritual vibe that is consistent with where we are mentally and emotionally. This is why you can feel when someone is not mentally present with you even if they are physically right there in front of you going through the motions.

In **Matthew 10:10** Jesus instructs his disciples not to take any bags for the journey. And this verse can be used as a metaphor for life concerning the importance of not carrying excess baggage as we walk this journey called life.

In this section of the *Soul Fast Journal*, called, **The Heart** you will take 10 days to fast from toxic emotions. You will be focusing on letting go of emotions that you still may subconsciously be holding on to that are pulling you in the direction of unhappiness, resentment, stagnation and hopelessness. Let's get started.

Here Are Some Selected Bible Scriptures
That You Can Feast On As You Fast From Toxic Emotions

3 John 1:2 Beloved, I wish above all things that you may prosper and be in health, even as your soul prospers.

Proverbs 4:23 Above all else, guard your heart, for everything you do flows from it.

Proverbs 17:22 A joyful heart is good medicine, But a broken spirit dries up the bon

Ecclesiastes 7:9 Do not be quickly provoked in your spirit, for anger resides in the lap of fools.

John 14:27 - Peace I leave with you, my peace I give unto you: not as the world giveth, give I unto you. Let not your heart be troubled, neither let it be afraid.

2 Corinthians 12:9 - And he said unto me, My grace is sufficient for thee: for my strength is made perfect in weakness. Most gladly therefore will I rather glory in my infirmities, that the power of Christ may rest upon me.

Matthew 11:28 - Come unto me, all ye that labor and are heavy laden, and I will give you rest.

Jeremiah 29:11 For I know the plans I have for you, declares the LORD, plans for welfare and not for evil, to give you a future and a hope.

Isaiah 61:3 To grant to those who mourn in Zion— to give them a beautiful headdress instead of ashes, the oil of gladness instead of mourning, the garment of praise instead of a faint spirit; that they may be called oaks of righteousness, the planting of the LORD, that he may be glorified.

Romans 8:1 There is therefore now no condemnation for those who are in Christ Jesus.

Philippians 4:6-7 Do not be anxious about anything, but in everything by prayer and supplication with thanksgiving let your requests be made known to God. And the peace of God, which surpasses all understanding, will guard your hearts and your minds in Christ Jesus.

Isaiah 54:17 - No weapon that is formed against thee shall prosper; and every tongue [that] shall rise against thee in judgment thou shalt condemn. This is the heritage of the servants of the LORD, and their righteousness is of me, saith the LORD.

Psalm 147:3 He heals the brokenhearted and binds up their wounds.

Jeremiah 17:9 "The heart is more deceitful than all else And is desperately sick; Who can understand it?

James 5:14 Is anyone among you sick? Then he must call for the elders of the church and they are to pray over him, anointing him with oil in the name of the Lord

Ephesians 4:26 "In your anger do not sin": Do not let the sun go down while you are still angry, 27 and do not give the devil a foothold.

Day 11

✸Today's Date: _____

Worksheet for Day 11

Fasting From Toxic Emotions

1. **Pray:** Start your day with prayer. Thank God for all of your blessings including the blessing of being able to see a brand, new day today. Give God the praise by telling God how great He is. Talk to God about whatever is on your heart this morning. Ask God to reveal any toxic emotions like: resentment, bitterness, hatred, envy, guilt, shame, regret, self-loathing, rejection, fear, apathy, loneliness, retaliation that you need to give over to God so that you can start detoxing from them and so that they do not embed themselves in your heart; poisoning your relationships, undermining your happiness, destroying great opportunities and eroding your health.

2. **Identify The Emotion That You Intend To Release So That You Can Be Free of The Toxic Effects Of That Emotion:**
   _____
   _____
   _____

3. **Release It:**
   Say: I Release …. _____
   (fill in the blank with the emotion that you are releasing).

4. **Renew A Right Spirit By Asking God To Cleanse Your Heart of The Toxic Emotion.**
   Pray: *God I Ask That You Cleanse My Heart Of…* (Fill In The Blank) _____
   _____ Show me how to let it go so that it does not create a stronghold for me. Show me the areas in my heart, personality, perspective, attitude, temperament and my reactions to people who hurt/upset/frustrate/anger me that make it harder than necessary to let this toxic emotion go. Show me how to feast on the medicinal benefits of a joyful heart (Proverbs 17:22) so that my spirit does not become broken or enslaved by toxic emotions and excess emotional baggage. In Jesus name, Amen!

5. **Select One of the Scriptures On Emotions. Meditate On Your Selected Scripture. Think About What God Is Saying To You Personally By Way Of This Scripture:**

6. **Declare:** Say your selected bible scripture out loud.

7. **Journal Space …** ✎

Following is your journal space. You can write down your thoughts, feelings, insights, prayers or anything else that you feel led to write. You can also write down any questions that you want to explore during your quiet time with God.

_____

_____
_____
_____
_____
_____
_____
_____
_____
_____
_____
_____
_____
_____
_____
_____
_____
_____
_____
_____
_____
_____
_____
_____
_____
_____
_____
_____
_____
_____

Day 12

✸Today's Date: _____

Worksheet for Day 12

Fasting From Toxic Emotions

1. **Pray:** Start your day with prayer. Thank God for all of your blessings including the blessing of being able to see a brand, new day today. Give God the praise by telling God how great He is. Talk to God about whatever is on your heart this morning. Ask God to reveal any toxic emotions like: resentment, bitterness, hatred, envy, guilt, shame, regret, self-loathing, rejection, fear, apathy, loneliness, retaliation that you need to give over to God so that you can start detoxing from them and so that they do not embed themselves in your heart; poisoning your relationships, undermining your happiness, destroying great opportunities and eroding your health.

2. **Identify The Emotion That You Intend To Release So That You Can Be Free of The Toxic Effects Of That Emotion:**

   _____
   _____
   _____

3. **Release It:**
   Say: I Release …. _____
   (fill in the blank with the emotion that you are releasing).

4. **Renew A Right Spirit By Asking God To Cleanse Your Heart of The Toxic Emotion.**
   Pray: *God I Ask That You Cleanse My Heart Of…* (Fill In The Blank) _____
   _____ Show me how to let it go so that it does not create a stronghold for me. Show me the areas in my heart, personality, perspective, attitude, temperament and my reactions to people who hurt/upset/frustrate/anger me that make it harder than necessary to let this toxic emotion go. Show me how to feast on the medicinal benefits of a joyful heart (Proverbs 17:22) so that my spirit does not become broken or enslaved by toxic emotions and excess emotional baggage. In Jesus name, Amen!

5. **Select One of the Scriptures On Emotions. Meditate On Your Selected Scripture. Think About What God Is Saying To You Personally By Way Of This Scripture:**

6. **Declare:** Say your selected bible scripture out loud.

7. **Journal Space …** 🖎

Following is your journal space. You can write down your thoughts, feelings, insights, prayers or anything else that you feel led to write. You can also write down any questions that you want to explore during your quiet time with God.

Day 13

✹Today's Date: _____

Worksheet for Day 13

Fasting From Toxic Emotions

1. **Pray:** Start your day with prayer. Thank God for all of your blessings including the blessing of being able to see a brand, new day today. Give God the praise by telling God how great He is. Talk to God about whatever is on your heart this morning. Ask God to reveal any toxic emotions like: resentment, bitterness, hatred, envy, guilt, shame, regret, self-loathing, rejection, fear, apathy, loneliness, retaliation that you need to give over to God so that you can start detoxing from them and so that they do not embed themselves in your heart; poisoning your relationships, undermining your happiness, destroying great opportunities and eroding your health.

2. **Identify The Emotion That You Intend To Release So That You Can Be Free of The Toxic Effects Of That Emotion:**

   _____
   _____
   _____

3. **Release It:**
   Say: I Release .... _____
   (fill in the blank with the emotion that you are releasing).

4. **Renew A Right Spirit By Asking God To Cleanse Your Heart of The Toxic Emotion.**
   Pray: *God I Ask That You Cleanse My Heart Of...* (Fill In The Blank) _____
   _____ Show me how to let it go so that it does not create a stronghold for me. Show me the areas in my heart, personality, perspective, attitude, temperament and my reactions to people who hurt/upset/frustrate/anger me that make it harder than necessary to let this toxic emotion go. Show me how to feast on the medicinal benefits of a joyful heart (Proverbs 17:22) so that my spirit does not become broken or enslaved by toxic emotions and excess emotional baggage. In Jesus name, Amen!

5. **Select One of the Scriptures On Emotions. Meditate On Your Selected Scripture. Think About What God Is Saying To You Personally By Way Of This Scripture:**

6. **Declare:** Say your selected bible scripture out loud.

7. **Journal Space ...** ✍

Following is your journal space. You can write down your thoughts, feelings, insights, prayers or anything else that you feel led to write. You can also write down any questions that you want to explore during your quiet time with God.

Day 14

✸Today's Date: _____

Worksheet for Day 14

Fasting From Toxic Emotions

1. **Pray:** Start your day with prayer. Thank God for all of your blessings including the blessing of being able to see a brand, new day today. Give God the praise by telling God how great He is. Talk to God about whatever is on your heart this morning. Ask God to reveal any toxic emotions like: resentment, bitterness, hatred, envy, guilt, shame, regret, self-loathing, rejection, fear, apathy, loneliness, retaliation that you need to give over to God so that you can start detoxing from them and so that they do not embed themselves in your heart; poisoning your relationships, undermining your happiness, destroying great opportunities and eroding your health.

2. **Identify The Emotion That You Intend To Release So That You Can Be Free of The Toxic Effects Of That Emotion:**
   _____
   _____
   _____

3. **Release It:**
   Say: I Release …. _____
   (fill in the blank with the emotion that you are releasing).

4. **Renew A Right Spirit By Asking God To Cleanse Your Heart of The Toxic Emotion.**
   Pray: *God I Ask That You Cleanse My Heart Of…* (Fill In The Blank) _____
   _____ Show me how to let it go so that it does not create a stronghold for me. Show me the areas in my heart, personality, perspective, attitude, temperament and my reactions to people who hurt/upset/frustrate/anger me that make it harder than necessary to let this toxic emotion go. Show me how to feast on the medicinal benefits of a joyful heart (Proverbs 17:22) so that my spirit does not become broken or enslaved by toxic emotions and excess emotional baggage. In Jesus name, Amen!

5. **Select One of the Scriptures On Emotions. Meditate On Your Selected Scripture. Think About What God Is Saying To You Personally By Way Of This Scripture:**

6. **Declare:** Say your selected bible scripture out loud.

7. **Journal Space …** ✍

Following is your journal space. You can write down your thoughts, feelings, insights, prayers or anything else that you feel led to write. You can also write down any questions that you want to explore during your quiet time with God.

_____

_____
_____
_____
_____
_____
_____
_____
_____
_____
_____
_____
_____
_____
_____
_____
_____
_____
_____
_____
_____
_____
_____
_____
_____
_____
_____

Day 15

❋Today's Date: _____

Worksheet for Day 15

Fasting From Toxic Emotions

1. **Pray:** Start your day with prayer. Thank God for all of your blessings including the blessing of being able to see a brand, new day today. Give God the praise by telling God how great He is. Talk to God about whatever is on your heart this morning. Ask God to reveal any toxic emotions like: resentment, bitterness, hatred, envy, guilt, shame, regret, self-loathing, rejection, fear, apathy, loneliness, retaliation that you need to give over to God so that you can start detoxing from them and so that they do not embed themselves in your heart; poisoning your relationships, undermining your happiness, destroying great opportunities and eroding your health.

2. **Identify The Emotion That You Intend To Release So That You Can Be Free of The Toxic Effects Of That Emotion:**

   _____

   _____

   _____

3. **Release It:**
   Say: I Release …. _____
   (fill in the blank with the emotion that you are releasing).

4. **Renew A Right Spirit By Asking God To Cleanse Your Heart of The Toxic Emotion.**
   Pray: *God I Ask That You Cleanse My Heart Of…* (Fill In The Blank) _____
   _____ Show me how to let it go so that it does not create a stronghold for me. Show me the areas in my heart, personality, perspective, attitude, temperament and my reactions to people who hurt/upset/frustrate/anger me that make it harder than necessary to let this toxic emotion go. Show me how to feast on the medicinal benefits of a joyful heart (Proverbs 17:22) so that my spirit does not become broken by toxic emotions and excess emotional baggage. In Jesus name, Amen!

5. **Select One of the Scriptures On Emotions. Meditate On Your Selected Scripture. Think About What God Is Saying To You Personally By Way Of This Scripture:**

6. **Declare:** Say your selected bible scripture out loud.

7. **Journal Space …** ✍

The Soul Fast Workbook. Copyright © 2017 by Cassandra Mack.

Following is your journal space. You can write down your thoughts, feelings, insights, prayers or anything else that you feel led to write. You can also write down any questions that you want to explore during your quiet time with God.

Don't Let Them Take Your Ice Cream

The Importance of Holding On To Your Joy

Remember when you were a kid and you heard the sound of the ice cream truck? *Shhhhh!* Don't tell anyone but I still get excited when I hear the ice cream truck because it brings me back to the carefree days of being a child.

The magic of the ice cream truck was this: No matter how bad or sad you felt in that moment or whatever you were in the middle of doing, when you heard the sound of the ice cream truck, it put a smile on your face and got your attention immediately.

For most of us, the ice cream truck had the power to make us smile, life our mood and warm our hearts with so much joyful anticipation that we could not wait to go outside and get some ice cream. In fact, the ice cream bell was so loud and distinctive that you knew it was coming before it actually arrived. *What was your favorite flavor?* Mine was a tossup between the ice cream sandwich and a chocolate cone with rainbow sprinkles.

Believe it or not, from a childhood point of view…there was power in the ice cream truck. As a child, the ice cream truck had the power to fill your heart with gladness as you contemplated which type of ice cream you were going to get. The ice cream struck had the power to deepen friendships because if you had a best friend and only one of you had money for ice cream, you would get the twin pop or the ice cream sandwich so that you could break the bar in half and each get a piece. Now if you were the bestest of best friends and declared yourself as blood brothers or sisters and only one of you had money, you would do the unthinkable: *Get one ice cream cone and take turns licking it, sprinkles and all.*

Believe it or not, as a child, the ice cream truck also gave you the power to stand because even if you were a mild-mannered kid who walked away from trouble, if the school bully tried to take your ice cream on the day when you were saving up all of your pennies, nickels and dimes to get your ice cream, even if you initially were scared and believed that you had no wins …on that day, the bully was in for the fight of his life. Know why? Because every kid above the age of three knows …. *Don't you dare try to take my ice cream!* You see where I'm going with this?

Did you know that in many ways your **Joy** is just like your ice cream? I like to think of my joy in the same way that I think about ice cream on a hot summer day… something that helps me bring a slice of contentment to my life, fills my heart with gladness, enables me to cool down when my emotions are hot and over the top and it takes me to my happy place, no matter what is trying to come against me.

Now I don't know about you, but I love ice cream and there are some days depending on what I am going through where I need it more than others. Reason being: Because on more days than not when people test my patience or do something so incredibly wicked that I have to literally sit on my hands to prevent myself from slapping the stupid off of them, I have to remind myself over and over again for my own well-being, that I cannot afford to let anyone **TAKE MY ICE CREAM.** Feel me? **Don't Let Anyone or anything steal your joy!**

For our own emotional wellbeing, we all have to get to a point in our lives where we guard our joy so vigilantly, that we never allow any person or circumstance to steal it. Proverbs 15:13 reminds us of this ...."*A joyful heart makes a cheerful face, but when the heart is sad, the spirit is broken.*"

Today, make up your mind to hold on to your joy. Don't let anyone steal your or break your spirit. Just like you trained your ear as a child to listen for the sound of the ice cream truck, you also have to train your heart and your mind by reading your Bible, spending time with God in prayer and do the little things that lift your spirit so that you can listen for the sound of joy. What does your joy sound like? Mine sounds like laughter, gratitude for the little things, peace of mind and taking authority over my emotional state. *What does your joy sound like?*

Psalms 118:24 tell us..." *This is the day that the Lord has made; let us rejoice and be glad in it.*" This means that just the simple fact that God saw fit to let you see another day is a reason enough to celebrate the *Present* and approach each day with a spirit of gratitude. You have the power to go get your ice cream any time you want to. You can even give some ice cream to somebody who's clearly unhappy or stressed and needs a little ice cream in their life a whole lot more than you do.

Never allow your heart to become so hardened by the disappointments of life, that you forfeit your joy. There are a whole lot of people in the graveyard who will never be able to hear the sound of the ice cream truck again. So, don't take your ice cream for granted! No matter your situation there is always a reason to rejoice in the day that the Lord has made.

- If you've got health issues, but you are still alive and kicking ...*Go get your ice cream!*
- If you've got money troubles, yet and still God made a way out of no way ...*Go get your ice cream!*
- If you've been feeling depressed and defeated but you're smiling as you read this ...*Go get your ice cream!*

Your ice cream belongs exclusively to you. Your ice cream represents your **JOY.** Now take a deep breath and **Declare** with expectation..."*This is the day that the Lord has made I WILL REJOICE and BE GLAD In It!*"

Day 16

✸Today's Date: _____

Worksheet for Day 16

Fasting From Toxic Emotions

1. **Pray:** Start your day with prayer. Thank God for all of your blessings including the blessing of being able to see a brand, new day today. Give God the praise by telling God how great He is. Talk to God about whatever is on your heart this morning. Ask God to reveal any toxic emotions like: resentment, bitterness, hatred, envy, guilt, shame, regret, self-loathing, rejection, fear, apathy, loneliness, retaliation that you need to give over to God so that you can start detoxing from them and so that they do not embed themselves in your heart; poisoning your relationships, undermining your happiness, destroying great opportunities and eroding your health.

2. **Identify The Emotion That You Intend To Release So That You Can Be Free of The Toxic Effects Of That Emotion:**
_____
_____
_____

3. **Release It:**
Say: I Release …. _____
(fill in the blank with the emotion that you are releasing).

4. **Renew A Right Spirit By Asking God To Cleanse Your Heart of The Toxic Emotion.**
Pray: *God I Ask That You Cleanse My Heart Of...* (Fill In The Blank) _____
_____ Show me how to let it go so that it does not create a stronghold for me. Show me the areas in my heart, personality, perspective, attitude, temperament and my reactions to people who hurt/upset/frustrate/anger me that make it harder than necessary to let this toxic emotion go. Show me how to feast on the medicinal benefits of a joyful heart (<u>Proverbs 17:22</u>) so that my spirit does not become broken or enslaved by toxic emotions and excess emotional baggage. In Jesus name, Amen!

5. **Select One of the Scriptures On Emotions. Meditate On Your Selected Scripture. Think About What God Is Saying To You Personally By Way Of This Scripture:**

6. **Declare:** Say your selected bible scripture out loud.

7. **Journal Space** … ✍

The Soul Fast Workbook. Copyright © 2017 by Cassandra Mack.

Following is your journal space. You can write down your thoughts, feelings, insights, prayers or anything else that you feel led to write. You can also write down any questions that you want to explore during your quiet time with God.

Day 17

✹Today's Date: _____

Worksheet for Day 17

Fasting From Toxic Emotions

1. **Pray:** Start your day with prayer. Thank God for all of your blessings including the blessing of being able to see a brand, new day today. Give God the praise by telling God how great He is. Talk to God about whatever is on your heart this morning. Ask God to reveal any toxic emotions like: resentment, bitterness, hatred, envy, guilt, shame, regret, self-loathing, rejection, fear, apathy, loneliness, retaliation that you need to give over to God so that you can start detoxing from them and so that they do not embed themselves in your heart; poisoning your relationships, undermining your happiness, destroying great opportunities and eroding your health.

2. **Identify The Emotion That You Intend To Release So That You Can Be Free of The Toxic Effects Of That Emotion:**

_____

_____

_____

3. **Release It:**
Say: I Release .... _____
(fill in the blank with the emotion that you are releasing).

4. **Renew A Right Spirit By Asking God To Cleanse Your Heart of The Toxic Emotion.**
Pray: *God I Ask That You Cleanse My Heart Of...* (Fill In The Blank) _____
_____ Show me how to let it go so that it does not create a stronghold for me. Show me the areas in my heart, personality, perspective, attitude, temperament and my reactions to people who hurt/upset/frustrate/anger me that make it harder than necessary to let this toxic emotion go. Show me how to feast on the medicinal benefits of a joyful heart (<u>Proverbs 17:22</u>) so that my spirit does not become broken or enslaved by toxic emotions and excess emotional baggage. In Jesus name, Amen!

5. **Select One of the Scriptures On Emotions. Meditate On Your Selected Scripture. Think About What God Is Saying To You Personally By Way Of This Scripture:**

6. **Declare:** Say your selected bible scripture out loud.

7. **Journal Space ...** 🖋

The Soul Fast Workbook. Copyright © 2017 by Cassandra Mack.

Following is your journal space. You can write down your thoughts, feelings, insights, prayers or anything else that you feel led to write. You can also write down any questions that you want to explore during your quiet time with God.

Day 18

✷Today's Date: _____

Worksheet for Day 18

Fasting From Toxic Emotions

1. **Pray:** Start your day with prayer. Thank God for all of your blessings including the blessing of being able to see a brand, new day today. Give God the praise by telling God how great He is. Talk to God about whatever is on your heart this morning. Ask God to reveal any toxic emotions like: resentment, bitterness, hatred, envy, guilt, shame, regret, self-loathing, rejection, fear, apathy, loneliness, retaliation that you need to give over to God so that you can start detoxing from them and so that they do not embed themselves in your heart; poisoning your relationships, undermining your happiness, destroying great opportunities and eroding your health.

2. **Identify The Emotion That You Intend To Release So That You Can Be Free of The Toxic Effects Of That Emotion:**

   _____
   _____
   _____

3. **Release It:**
   Say: I Release …. _____
   (fill in the blank with the emotion that you are releasing).

4. **Renew A Right Spirit By Asking God To Cleanse Your Heart of The Toxic Emotion.**
   Pray: *God I Ask That You Cleanse My Heart Of…* (Fill In The Blank) _____ Show me how to let it go so that it does not create a stronghold for me. Show me the areas in my heart, personality, perspective, attitude, temperament and my reactions to people who hurt/upset/frustrate/anger me that make it harder than necessary to let this toxic emotion go. Show me how to feast on the medicinal benefits of a joyful heart (Proverbs 17:22) so that my spirit does not become broken or enslaved by toxic emotions and excess emotional baggage. In Jesus name, Amen!

5. **Select One of the Scriptures On Emotions. Meditate On Your Selected Scripture. Think About What God Is Saying To You Personally By Way Of This Scripture:**

6. **Declare:** Say your selected bible scripture out loud.

7. **Journal Space …** ✍

Following is your journal space. You can write down your thoughts, feelings, insights, prayers or anything else that you feel led to write. You can also write down any questions that you want to explore during your quiet time with God.

_____

_____

_____

_____

_____

_____

_____

_____

_____

_____

_____

_____

_____

_____

_____

_____

_____

_____

_____

_____

_____

_____

_____

_____

_____

_____

_____

Day 19

✹Today's Date: _____

Worksheet for Day 19

Fasting From Toxic Emotions

1. **Pray:** Start your day with prayer. Thank God for all of your blessings including the blessing of being able to see a brand, new day today. Give God the praise by telling God how great He is. Talk to God about whatever is on your heart this morning. Ask God to reveal any toxic emotions like: resentment, bitterness, hatred, envy, guilt, shame, regret, self-loathing, rejection, fear, apathy, loneliness, retaliation that you need to give over to God so that you can start detoxing from them and so that they do not embed themselves in your heart; poisoning your relationships, undermining your happiness, destroying great opportunities and eroding your health.

2. **Identify The Emotion That You Intend To Release So That You Can Be Free of The Toxic Effects Of That Emotion:**

   _____
   _____
   _____

3. **Release It:**
   Say: I Release .... _____
   (fill in the blank with the emotion that you are releasing).

4. **Renew A Right Spirit By Asking God To Cleanse Your Heart of The Toxic Emotion.**
   Pray: *God I Ask That You Cleanse My Heart Of...* (Fill In The Blank)
   _____ Show me how to let it go so that it does not create a stronghold for me. Show me the areas in my heart, personality, perspective, attitude, temperament and my reactions to people who hurt/upset/frustrate/anger me that make it harder than necessary to let this toxic emotion go. Show me how to feast on the medicinal benefits of a joyful heart (Proverbs 17:22) so that my spirit does not become broken or enslaved by toxic emotions and excess emotional baggage. In Jesus name, Amen!

5. **Select One of the Scriptures On Emotions. Meditate On Your Selected Scripture. Think About What God Is Saying To You Personally By Way Of This Scripture:**

6. **Declare:** Say your selected bible scripture out loud.

7. **Journal Space ...** ✍

Following is your journal space. You can write down your thoughts, feelings, insights, prayers or anything else that you feel led to write. You can also write down any questions that you want to explore during your quiet time with God.

Day 20

✹Today's Date: _____

Worksheet for Day 20

Fasting From Toxic Emotions

1. **Pray:** Start your day with prayer. Thank God for all of your blessings including the blessing of being able to see a brand, new day today. Give God the praise by telling God how great He is. Talk to God about whatever is on your heart this morning. Ask God to reveal any toxic emotions like: resentment, bitterness, hatred, envy, guilt, shame, regret, self-loathing, rejection, fear, apathy, loneliness, retaliation that you need to give over to God so that you can start detoxing from them and so that they do not embed themselves in your heart; poisoning your relationships, undermining your happiness, destroying great opportunities and eroding your health.

2. **Identify The Emotion That You Intend To Release So That You Can Be Free of The Toxic Effects Of That Emotion:**
   _____
   _____
   _____

3. **Release It:**
   Say: I Release …. _____
   (fill in the blank with the emotion that you are releasing).

4. **Renew A Right Spirit By Asking God To Cleanse Your Heart of The Toxic Emotion.**
   Pray: *God I Ask That You Cleanse My Heart Of…* (Fill In The Blank) _____ Show me how to let it go so that it does not create a stronghold for me. Show me the areas in my heart, personality, perspective, attitude, temperament and my reactions to people who hurt/upset/frustrate/anger me that make it harder than necessary to let this toxic emotion go. Show me how to feast on the medicinal benefits of a joyful heart (Proverbs 17:22) so that my spirit does not become broken or enslaved by toxic emotions and excess emotional baggage. In Jesus name, Amen!

5. **Select One of the Scriptures On Emotions. Meditate On Your Selected Scripture. Think About What God Is Saying To You Personally By Way Of This Scripture:**

6. **Declare:** Say your selected bible scripture out loud.

7. **Journal Space …** ✍

The Soul Fast Workbook. Copyright © 2017 by Cassandra Mack.

Following is your journal space. You can write down your thoughts, feelings, insights, prayers or anything else that you feel led to write. You can also write down any questions that you want to explore during your quiet time with God.

Your Check In

✹ Good job!

You made it through 20 days of the soul fast. I knew you could do it.

The mere fact that you took 10 days to fast from toxic emotions is another accomplishment on your journey to a prosperous soul. Here's why: You've now empowered yourself to change the quality of your emotional life by way of searching your heart.

(Psalm 139:23)

1.   Did you fast from toxic emotions for the entire 10-day period or did you skip a day? What was this experience like for you?

2.   Did you complete your worksheets each day? What were you surprised to find yourself writing about most frequently?

3.   Did you have any insights, discoveries, revelations or breakthroughs during this time?

4.   What do you believe God is saying to you about your emotional life, now that you've taken some time out to detox from toxic emotions?

5.   Are there any other issues that you consider significant to your emotional wellbeing that you feel led to continue working on?

Section 3
The Will
Fasting From Choices That Lead To Regret & Self-Sabotage

The Will: Fasting From Choices That Lead To Regret & Self-Sabotage

"Choose Life" (Deuteronomy 30:19)

I want to tell you a story about a man who I am going to call Jimmy, which is not his real name, to illustrate the importance of becoming intentional about our choices so that we don't make too many short-sighted decisions that bring us short-term gain but that we end up paying for residually when it's all said and done. This section of *The Soul Fast Workbook* is all about learning how to choose life in every situation so that we don't keep walking down paths that lead us into temptation, regret and self-sabotage.

... At thirty-six years old, Jimmy was frustrated with his life. His career was at a standstill. His credit was bad due to overspending. He neglected to pay his bills on time. He had an eviction notice on his front door. This meant he now had to quickly come up with a plan for alternate lodging as he wrapped his mind around his new reality that he was going to be without a home. Jimmy was stressed beyond comprehension. His life was spiraling downhill fast. He had an ex-wife he was paying alimony to. Two baby's mamas in the mix. And to top it all off, the woman whom he was casually sleeping with was three months pregnant with his child. It was at that moment that Jimmy realized his life was in shambles. Everything that he had ever planned for, hoped for and worked for was crumbling apart at his feet. This was not the kind of life that Jimmy imagined he would be living. But like it or not, this was Jimmy's life. And in the midst of his disbelief and growing despair, the one thing that Jimmy neglected to remind himself of was this: *It was Jimmy's own free will choices that landed him on this path.* Jimmy was a man in denial. He had a really bad habit of choosing choices that felt good in the moment but that often came with residual ramifications that he wasn't fully prepared to pay. But, ready or not Jimmy was reaping the whirlwind of the free will winds that he had sown. However, Jimmy was too busy blaming and complaining; to step back and self-evaluate so that he could honestly assess just how it was he got here.

Every experience, every relationship, every aspect of your adult life is directly related to a choice you either made or failed to make at some point in time. Very rarely do things just happen to us without there first being a choice that we either made or neglected to make. The law of cause and effect teaches us that every choice we make today has implications on our tomorrow, our next week, our next year ...and sometimes the rest of our lives. The Bible puts it this way in <u>Galatians 6: 7</u> *"Be not deceived; God is not mocked: for whatsoever a man sows, that shall he also reap."*

There is no way around this very real facet of life because every choice we make or neglect to make is attached to a set of outcomes, even if we can't foresee them. For example: if you steal from your job and you get caught, not only does this choice affect your employment, which affects your ability to bring in an income. This choice can also affect your freedom if you are prosecuted for theft. Now if you are married with kids, then being away from your family will affect your spouse and children and your spouse may choose to file for a divorce and move on without you. Now you have no job, no income, no spouse, no access to your kids and more than likely you will be homeless, because you cannot pay your rent or mortgage while you are in jail without an income.

Most people don't like to admit this, but more often than not, with very few exceptions, the negative situations that we find ourselves in can usually be traced back to a choice that we either made or failed to make. Can you think of a choice you made or failed to make that yielded negative consequences? Speaking for myself, I can think of lots of reckless and foolish choices that I've made in which I've had to reap the consequences. And even though each of us can learn from our mistakes and come back stronger from virtually any setback, it's even better to choose well from the onset whenever two paths are laid before us, because it's the little decisions that determine who we become and where we end up in life. *It's the little foxes that spoil the vine.* (Song of Solomon 2:15)

Each and every day we get to create our reality with the choices that we make. For example: Every time you dwell on self-defeating thoughts, you are creating your mental reality and putting the cause of insecurity and anxiety into effect. Every time you act out in anger or elect to remain in a prolonged state of sorrow, you are creating your emotional reality and putting the cause of stress and depression into effect. Every time you enter into a relationship with someone who does not value you and who's completely okay with using you, you are creating your relationship reality and putting the cause of dysfunction and heartache into effect. Every time you become complacent on your job and neglect to invest in your career, you are creating your professional reality and putting the cause of career stagnation into effect. Every time you allow your credit card spending to get out of hand, you are creating your financial reality and putting the cause of debt into effect. Like it or not, most of the circumstances that exist in our lives are the direct result of a choice that we either made or failed to make. Hosea 8:7 puts it this way ..." *They sow the wind and reap the whirlwind.*" So, the reality of life is this: When we find ourselves in an undesirable situation that could have been avoided if we had made a different choice, then more often than not, we are reaping the whirlwind of the initial wind that we put into effect by way of our original choice.

Many people have conditioned themselves to blame something outside of their own adult choices for the aspects of their lives that they regret or are unhappy with. They blame a difficult childhood, the job, the ex-husband, baby mama, lack of education or anything else that can be used as an excuse to not take personal responsibility for their adult choices. I have been guilty of this myself. But once we realize the power behind every single choice we make, then it's incumbent upon us to start thinking more long term about the kinds of choices we make and the possible effects of our decisions or lack thereof.

If you want to change the conditions in your life, start by changing some of your choices. Learn to think beyond today. Take the long view before making a decision. You owe it to yourself to not only think about the immediate outcome of a particular choice, but also how it may impact your life in the future.

Each and every day, there are choices in life that are set before us (Deuteronomy 30:19), and we get to decide how we're going to live our lives. However, the key to choosing life when two opposing paths are set before us, is to make choices that are in line with our values, our goals, the knowledge, wisdom and understanding that we gain from reading the Bible and that are likely to lead to fruitful outcomes.

This section of *The Soul Fast Workbook* will deal with the *Will* – which is the seat of our choices. For the next 10 days, you will be learning how to detox from counterproductive choices so that you can figure out whether the choices that you're making are producing good fruit in your life or leading you down the path of fruitlessness and regret.

Here Are Some Selected Bible Scriptures That You Can Feast On As You Fast From Counterproductive Choices

Deuteronomy 30:19 - I call heaven and earth to record this day against you, [that] I have set before you life and death, blessing and cursing: therefore choose life, that both thou and thy seed may live

Proverbs 3:5-6 Trust in the Lord with all your heart; do not depend on your own understanding. Seek his will in all you do, and he will show you which path to take.

2 Timothy 1:7 For God has not given us the spirit of fear; but of power, and of love, and of a sound mind.

Proverbs 8:14 Counsel and sound judgment are mine; I have insight, I have power.

Song of Solomon 2:15 Catch us the foxes, the little foxes, that spoil the vines: for our vines have tender grapes.

1 Corinthians 10:13 No temptation has overtaken you except what is common to mankind. And God is faithful; he will not let you be tempted beyond what you can bear. But when you are tempted, he will also provide a way out so that you can endure it.

Ephesians 5:15-16 Be very careful, then, how you live—not as unwise but as wise, making the most of every opportunity, because the days are evil.

James 1:5 If any of you lacks wisdom, you should ask God, who gives generously to all without finding fault, and it will be given to you.

Colossians 4:5-6 Be wise in the way you act toward outsiders; make the most of every opportunity. Let your conversation be always full of grace, seasoned with salt, so that you may know how to answer everyone.

Matthew 6:21 For where your treasure is, there will your heart be also.

Proverbs 22: 1 A good name is more desirable than great riches; to be esteemed is better than silver or gold.

Romans 13:8 Let no debt remain outstanding, except the continuing debt to love one another, for whoever loves others has fulfilled the law.

Psalm 90:12 Teach us to number our days that we may gain a heart of wisdom.

Proverbs 15:33 Wisdom's instruction is to fear the Lord, and humility comes before honor.

Proverbs 15:22 Without counsel purposes are disappointed: but in the multitude of counselors they are established.

Proverbs 29:18 Where there is no vision, the people perish: but he that keepeth the law, happy is he.

Luke 14: 28 For which of you, intending to build a tower, sitteth not down first and counteth the cost, whether he have sufficient to finish it?

Proverbs 6:6-8 Go to the ant, you sluggard; consider its ways and be wise! It has no commander, no overseer or ruler yet it stores its provisions in summer and gathers its food at harvest.

Genesis 3: 1 Now the serpent was craftier than any of the wild animals the LORD God had made. He said to the woman, "Did God really say, 'You must not eat from any tree in the garden'?"

Proverbs 21:17 Those who love pleasure become poor; those who love wine and luxury will never be rich.

Proverbs 15:27 Greed brings grief to the whole family, but those who hate bribes will live.

Proverbs 3:27 Do not withhold good from those who deserve it when it's in your power to help them.

Joshua 24:15 If it is disagreeable in your sight to serve the LORD, choose for yourselves today whom you will serve: whether the gods which your fathers served which were beyond the River, or the gods of the Amorites in whose land you are living; but as for me and my house, we will serve the LORD.

Proverbs 3:31 Do not envy a man of violence and do not choose any of his ways.

Matthew 7: 7-8 Ask and it will be given to you; seek and you will find; knock and the door will be opened to you. For everyone who asks receives; the one who seeks finds; and to the one who knocks, the door will be opened.

Day 21

✸ Today's Date: _____

Worksheet for Day 21

Fasting From Counterproductive Choices

1. **Pray:** Start your day with prayer. Thank and praise God for all that He has done for you; including blessing you with a brand-new day of life. Talk to God about whatever is on your mind. Ask God for wisdom, clarity, guidance and direction. Ask God to show you any areas in your life where you might be making choices that are not in alignment with His plan for your life and that are working against your long-term success and wellbeing.

2. **Identify A Situation Where You Need To Make A Choice. Then Map Out Your Decision On Paper, So That You Can Choose Wisely:**
I need to make a choice about... _____
I need to make a decision about this issue because _____
(My choice is between the following options)
Choice A _____ or, Choice B _____
Since I want to *Choose Wisely* in this situation and do what's right. I will pray on it and allow God to direct my path because He always knows what's best for me. Furthermore, I don't have to waiver through my dilemma/problem/issue alone. Instead, if I need to seek wise counsel I can call: _____

3. **I Am Making The Choice To Choose Life:** (Deuteronomy 30:19) What actions do you need to take in order to choose life in this situation?

4. **Jot Down One of The Selected Scriptures That You Feel Led To Mediate On or You Can Use Another Bible Verse That Speaks To Your Situation**
_____
_____
_____

5. **Meditate On Your Selected Scripture and Think About What God Is Saying To You Personally By Way Of This Scripture:**

6. **Declare:** *I am* (say your name) and then say your bible scripture out loud.

7. **Journal Space ...** ✍
Following is your journal space. You can write down your thoughts, feelings, insights, prayers or anything else that you feel led to write. You can also write down any questions that you want to explore during your quiet time with God.

The Soul Fast Workbook. Copyright © 2017 by Cassandra Mack.

Day 22

✹Today's Date: _____

Worksheet for Day 22

Fasting From Counterproductive Choices

1. **Pray:** Start your day with prayer. Thank and praise God for all that He has done for you; including blessing you with a brand-new day of life. Talk to God about whatever is on your mind. Ask God for wisdom, clarity, guidance and direction. Ask God to show you any areas in your life where you might be making choices that are not in alignment with His plan for your life and that are working against your long-term success and wellbeing.

2. **Identify A Situation Where You Need To Make A Choice and Then Think Map It Out On Paper So That You Can Choose Wisely:**

I need to make a choice about... _____

I need to make a decision about this because _____

(My choice is between the following options)

<u>Choice A</u> _____ or, <u>Choice B</u> _____

Since I want to *Choose Wisely* in this situation and do what's right. I will pray on it and allow God to direct my path because He always knows what's best for me. Furthermore, I don't have to waiver through my dilemma/problem/issue alone. Instead, if I need to seek wise counsel I can call: _____

1. **I Am Making The Choice To Choose Life:** (<u>Deuteronomy 30:19</u>) What actions do you need to take in order to choose life in this situation?

2. **Jot Down One of The Selected Scriptures That You Feel Led To Mediate On or You Can Use Another Bible Verse That Speaks To Your Situation**

_____

_____

_____

3. **Meditate On Your Selected Scripture and Think About What God Is Saying To You Personally By Way Of This Scripture:**

4. **Declare:** *I am* (say your name) and then say your bible scripture out loud.

5. **Journal Space ...** 🖎

Following is your journal space. You can write down your thoughts, feelings, insights, prayers or anything else that you feel led to write. You can also write down any questions that you want to explore during your quiet time with God.

The Soul Fast Workbook. Copyright © 2017 by Cassandra Mack.

Day 23

✷ Today's Date: _____

Worksheet for Day 23

Fasting From Counterproductive Choices

1. **Pray:** Start your day with prayer. Thank and praise God for all that He has done for you; including blessing you with a brand-new day of life. Talk to God about whatever is on your mind. Ask God for wisdom, clarity, guidance and direction. Ask God to show you any areas in your life where you might be making choices that are not in alignment with His plan for your life and that are working against your long-term success and wellbeing.

2. **Identify A Situation Where You Need To Make A Choice and Then Map It Out On Paper So That You Can Choose Wisely:**
I need to make a choice about... _____
I need to make a decision about this because _____
(My choice is between the following options)
Choice A _____ or, Choice B _____
Since I want to *Choose Wisely* in this situation and do what's right. I will pray on it and allow God to direct my path because He always knows what's best for me. Furthermore, I don't have to waiver through my dilemma/problem/issue alone. Instead, if I need to seek wise counsel I can call: _____

3. **I Am Making The Choice To Choose Life:** (Deuteronomy 30:19) What actions do you need to take in order to choose life in this situation?

4. **Jot Down One of The Selected Scriptures That You Feel Led To Mediate On or You Can Use Another Bible Verse That Speaks To Your Situation**
_____
_____
_____

5. **Meditate On Your Selected Scripture and Think About What God Is Saying To You Personally By Way Of This Scripture:**

6. **Declare:** *I am* (say your name) and then say your bible scripture out loud.

7. **Journal Space ...** ✍
Following is your journal space. You can write down your thoughts, feelings, insights, prayers or anything else that you feel led to write. You can also write down any questions that you want to explore during your quiet time with God.

The Soul Fast Workbook. Copyright © 2017 by Cassandra Mack.

The Soul Fast Workbook. Copyright © 2017 by Cassandra Mack.
P. 91

Day 24

✺Today's Date: _____

Worksheet for Day 24

Fasting From Counterproductive Choices

1. **Pray:** Start your day with prayer. Thank and praise God for all that He has done for you; including blessing you with a brand-new day of life. Talk to God about whatever is on your mind. Ask God for wisdom, clarity, guidance and direction. Ask God to show you any areas in your life where you might be making choices that are not in alignment with His plan for your life and that are working against your long-term success and wellbeing.

2. **Identify A Situation Where You Need To Make A Choice and Then Map It Out On Paper So That You Can Choose Wisely:**
I need to make a choice about... _____
I need to make a decision about this because _____
(My choice is between the following options)
Choice A _____ or, Choice B _____
Since I want to *Choose Wisely* in this situation and do what's right. I will pray on it and allow God to direct my path because He always knows what's best for me. Furthermore, I don't have to waiver through my dilemma/problem/issue alone. Instead, if I need to seek wise counsel I can call: _____

3. **I Am Making The Choice To Choose Life:** (Deuteronomy 30:19) What actions do you need to take in order to choose life in this situation?

4. **Jot Down One of The Selected Scriptures That You Feel Led To Mediate On or You Can Use Another Bible Verse That Speaks To Your Situation**
_____
_____
_____

5. **Meditate On Your Selected Scripture and Think About What God Is Saying To You Personally By Way Of This Scripture:**

6. **Declare:** *I am (say your name)* and then say your bible scripture out loud.

7. **Journal Space ...** ✍
Following is your journal space. You can write down your thoughts, feelings, insights, prayers or anything else that you feel led to write. You can also write down any questions that you want to explore during your quiet time with God.

Day 25

✽Today's Date: _____

Worksheet for Day 25

Fasting From Counterproductive Choices

1. **Pray:** Start your day with prayer. Thank and praise God for all that He has done for you; including blessing you with a brand-new day of life. Talk to God about whatever is on your mind. Ask God for wisdom, clarity, guidance and direction. Ask God to show you any areas in your life where you might be making choices that are not in alignment with His plan for your life and that are working against your long-term success and wellbeing.

2. **Identify A Situation Where You Need To Make A Choice and Then Map It Out On Paper So That You Can Choose Wisely:**
I need to make a choice about... _____
I need to make a decision about this because _____
(My choice is between the following options)
Choice A _____ or, Choice B _____
Since I want to *Choose Wisely* in this situation and do what's right. I will pray on it and allow God to direct my path because He always knows what's best for me. Furthermore, I don't have to waiver through my dilemma/problem/issue alone. Instead, if I need to seek wise counsel I can call: _____

3. **I Am Making The Choice To Choose Life:** (Deuteronomy 30:19) What actions do you need to take in order to choose life in this situation?

4. **Jot Down One of The Selected Scriptures That You Feel Led To Mediate On or You Can Use Another Bible Verse That Speaks To Your Situation**
_____
_____
_____

5. **Meditate On Your Selected Scripture and Think About What God Is Saying To You Personally By Way Of This Scripture:**

6. **Declare:** *I am* (say your name) and then say your bible scripture out loud.

7. **Journal Space ...** ✍
Following is your journal space. You can write down your thoughts, feelings, insights, prayers or anything else that you feel led to write. You can also write down any questions that you want to explore during your quiet time with God.

The Soul Fast Workbook. Copyright © 2017 by Cassandra Mack.

Hot Peas & Butter

The Butt Whipping Price of Purpose: Are You Willing To Pay It?

When you were a child, did you ever play the game: *Hot Peas and Butter*? Hot peas and butter was a game in which the person who is "*it*" hides a belt and asks the rest of the players to try and find it. As each player looks for the belt, the person who hid the belt aka "it" has to let the players know if they are getting HOT (in close proximity to the belt), WARM (in the vicinity of the belt but not as close as those who are hot), or COLD (completely missing the mark and nowhere near the belt).

And when one of the players finds the belt he or she has to shout: *Hot peas and butter, come and get your supper!*" and all of the other players have to run back to base before they got their butts whipped with the belt. Now *Hot Peas and Butter* is not a game for the super sensitive, the hyper politically correct, the easily offended, the prissy type who doesn't want to get their clothes dirty or those who did not have the kind of urban grit to roll up their sleeves and take one for the team.

Granted in today's times kids may not be able to play *Hot Pease and Butter* because it might be construed as abuse. Understandable. Things are different today. But if you grew up in an urban area in the 70's, 80's or early 90's, then this was just one of many sidewalk, street corner games that you played as a kid. The object of the game was to find the hidden belt, which was the supper to the, *Hot Peas and Butter.*

Unfortunately, as we get older a lot of us become like the kids who were stuck in the cold zone of the game where they were nowhere near the hidden belt. In other words, we have hidden gifts, underutilized talents and untapped abilities that we are hiding and allowing to grow lukewarm or cold. And just like the kids in *Hot Peas and Butter* who were looking for that hidden belt, some of us are getting warmer (closer to our purpose). Others are getting hot (right in the midst of our purpose). And then there are those of us who are getting colder with each passing day (because we've lost sight of our purpose) And believe it or not, some of us are afraid to look for the belt because the last time we tried to do something purposeful, and completely out of our comfort zone, we got our butts whipped with rejection or self-doubt or feelings of inadequacy. However just like in the game of *Hot Peas and Butter,* no matter how far off we are the object of the game is to find the hidden belt. The reason so many of us are afraid to look for the belt is because we tend to associate belts with butt whippings, but the higher purpose of the belt is to gird us with truth (Ephesians 6:14) so much truth that it becomes a piece of spiritual armor against the schemes and tactics of the enemy. So, there's no need to be afraid of the belt, and sometimes we have to get our butts whipped with truth in order to self-reflect and look at the areas in our lives where we are out of order.

See the thing about looking for the belt like in the game, *Hot Peas and Butter"* is you really can't uncover the fullness of your purpose without an occasional truth whipping. Why? Because nothing worthwhile comes easy. There's a butt whipping price we have to pay in order to live our dreams and reach our goals and it's called...blood, sweat and tears. But you know what? It really doesn't matter if you get your butt whipped on your way to your purpose, as long as you stay in the game.

If you really want to unlock the things that make you awesome and live life from your fearfully and wonderfully made place, then you've got to get to the point in your life where even if you get your butt whipped, you're still not letting go of God, because God won't let go of you. And as hard as this might be to digest, you can't get your supper unless you risk a butt whipping. You've got to find the belt. The belt doesn't come to you on a silver platter, but God will let you know when you're on target and when you've missed the mark.

So, as you get back in the game of life and you go about looking for that belt: Are you getting HOT, are you getting WARM or have you completely gone COLD and given up?

Always remember that there's power in your purpose, but you can't find it unless you look for the belt. *Hot peas and butter, come and get your supper.*

Romans 9:17 reminds us of this.... *"I raised you up for this very purpose, that I might display my power in you and that my name might be proclaimed in all the earth."*

God wants to raise us up for greatness, wholeness, destiny and purpose, but it's up to each and every one of us to make the **choice** to stop running from the belt.

.

✹ Today's Date: _____

Worksheet for Day 26

Fasting From Counterproductive Choices

1. **Pray:** Start your day with prayer. Thank and praise God for all that He has done for you; including blessing you with a brand-new day of life. Talk to God about whatever is on your mind. Ask God for wisdom, clarity, guidance and direction. Ask God to show you any areas in your life where you might be making choices that are not in alignment with His plan for your life and that are working against your long-term success and wellbeing.

2. **Identify A Situation Where You Need To Make A Choice and Then Map It Out On Paper So That You Can Choose Wisely:**
I need to make a choice about... _____
I need to make a decision about this because _____
(My choice is between the following options)
<u>Choice A</u> _____ or, <u>Choice B</u> _____
Since I want to *Choose Wisely* in this situation and do what's right. I will pray on it and allow God to direct my path because He always knows what's best for me. Furthermore, I don't have to waiver through my dilemma/problem/issue alone. Instead, if I need to seek wise counsel I can call: _____

3. **I Am Making The Choice To Choose Life:** (<u>Deuteronomy 30:19</u>) What actions do you need to take in order to choose life in this situation?

4. **Jot Down One of The Selected Scriptures That You Feel Led To Mediate On or You Can Use Another Bible Verse That Speaks To Your Situation**

_____

_____

_____

5. **Meditate On Your Selected Scripture and Think About What God Is Saying To You Personally By Way Of This Scripture:**

6. **Declare:** *I am* (say your name) and then say your bible scripture out loud.

7. **Journal Space ...** ✍
Following is your journal space. You can write down your thoughts, feelings, insights, prayers or anything else that you feel led to write. You can also write down any questions that you want to explore during your quiet time with God.

The Soul Fast Workbook. Copyright © 2017 by Cassandra Mack.

Day 27

Worksheet for Day 27

Fasting From Counterproductive Choices

1. **Pray:** Start your day with prayer. Thank and praise God for all that He has done for you; including blessing you with a brand-new day of life. Talk to God about whatever is on your mind. Ask God for wisdom, clarity, guidance and direction. Ask God to show you any areas in your life where you might be making choices that are not in alignment with His plan for your life and that are working against your long-term success and wellbeing.

2. **Identify A Situation Where You Need To Make A Choice and Then Map It Out On Paper So That You Can Choose Wisely:**
I need to make a choice about... _____
I need to make a decision about this because _____
(My choice is between the following options)
Choice A _____ or, Choice B _____
Since I want to *Choose Wisely* in this situation and do what's right. I will pray on it and allow God to direct my path because He always knows what's best for me. Furthermore, I don't have to waiver through my dilemma/problem/issue alone. Instead, if I need to seek wise counsel I can call: _____

3. **I Am Making The Choice To Choose Life:** (Deuteronomy 30:19) What actions do you need to take in order to choose life in this situation?

4. **Jot Down One of The Selected Scriptures That You Feel Led To Mediate On or You Can Use Another Bible Verse That Speaks To Your Situation**

_____

_____

_____

5. **Meditate On Your Selected Scripture and Think About What God Is Saying To You Personally By Way Of This Scripture:**

6. **Declare:** *I am* (say your name) and then say your bible scripture out loud.

7. **Journal Space ...** ✍
Following is your journal space. You can write down your thoughts, feelings, insights, prayers or anything else that you feel led to write. You can also write down any questions that you want to explore during your quiet time with God.

The Soul Fast Workbook. Copyright © 2017 by Cassandra Mack.

Day 28

✹Today's Date: _____

Worksheet for Day 28

Fasting From Counterproductive Choices

1. **Pray:** Start your day with prayer. Thank and praise God for all that He has done for you; including blessing you with a brand-new day of life. Talk to God about whatever is on your mind. Ask God for wisdom, clarity, guidance and direction. Ask God to show you any areas in your life where you might be making choices that are not in alignment with His plan for your life and that are working against your long-term success and wellbeing.

2. **Identify A Situation Where You Need To Make A Choice and Then Map It Out On Paper So That You Can Choose Wisely:**
   I need to make a choice about... _____
   I need to make a decision about this because _____
   (My choice is between the following options)
   <u>Choice A</u> _____ or, <u>Choice B</u> _____
   Since I want to *Choose Wisely* in this situation and do what's right. I will pray on it and allow God to direct my path because He always knows what's best for me. Furthermore, I don't have to waiver through my dilemma/problem/issue alone. Instead, if I need to seek wise counsel I can call: _____

3. **I Am Making The Choice To Choose Life:** (<u>Deuteronomy 30:19</u>) What actions do you need to take in order to choose life in this situation?

4. **Jot Down One of The Selected Scriptures That You Feel Led To Mediate On or You Can Use Another Bible Verse That Speaks To Your Situation**
   _____
   _____
   _____

5. **Meditate On Your Selected Scripture and Think About What God Is Saying To You Personally By Way Of This Scripture:**

6. **Declare:** *I am* (say your name) and then say your bible scripture out loud.

7. **Journal Space ...** ✍
   Following is your journal space. You can write down your thoughts, feelings, insights, prayers or anything else that you feel led to write. You can also write down any questions that you want to explore during your quiet time with God.

Day 29

✹Today's Date: _____

Worksheet for Day 29

Fasting From Counterproductive Choices

1. **Pray:** Start your day with prayer. Thank and praise God for all that He has done for you; including blessing you with a brand-new day of life. Talk to God about whatever is on your mind. Ask God for wisdom, clarity, guidance and direction. Ask God to show you any areas in your life where you might be making choices that are not in alignment with His plan for your life and that are working against your long-term success and wellbeing.

2. **Identify A Situation Where You Need To Make A Choice and Then Map It Out On Paper So That You Can Choose Wisely:**
I need to make a choice about... _____
I need to make a decision about this because _____
(My choice is between the following options)
<u>Choice A</u> _____ or, <u>Choice B</u> _____
Since I want to *Choose Wisely* in this situation and do what's right. I will pray on it and allow God to direct my path because He always knows what's best for me. Furthermore, I don't have to waiver through my dilemma/problem/issue alone. Instead, if I need to seek wise counsel I can call: _____

3. **I Am Making The Choice To Choose Life:** (<u>Deuteronomy 30:19</u>) What actions do you need to take in order to choose life in this situation?

4. **Jot Down One of The Selected Scriptures That You Feel Led To Mediate On or You Can Use Another Bible Verse That Speaks To Your Situation**
_____
_____
_____

5. **Meditate On Your Selected Scripture and Think About What God Is Saying To You Personally By Way Of This Scripture:**

6. **Declare:** *I am* (say your name) and then say your bible scripture out loud.

7. **Journal Space ...** ✍
Following is your journal space. You can write down your thoughts, feelings, insights, prayers or anything else that you feel led to write. You can also write down any questions that you want to explore during your quiet time with God.

Day 30

✸Today's Date: _____

Worksheet for Day 30

Fasting From Counterproductive Choices

1. **Pray:** Start your day with prayer. Thank and praise God for all that He has done for you; including blessing you with a brand-new day of life. Talk to God about whatever is on your mind. Ask God for wisdom, clarity, guidance and direction. Ask God to show you any areas in your life where you might be making choices that are not in alignment with His plan for your life and that are working against your long-term success and wellbeing.

2. **Identify A Situation Where You Need To Make A Choice and Then Map It Out On Paper So That You Can Choose Wisely:**
   I need to make a choice about... _____
   I need to make a decision about this because _____
   (My choice is between the following options)
   Choice A _____ or, Choice B _____
   Since I want to *Choose Wisely* in this situation and do what's right. I will pray on it and allow God to direct my path because He always knows what's best for me. Furthermore, I don't have to waiver through my dilemma/problem/issue alone. Instead, if I need to seek wise counsel I can call: _____

3. **I Am Making The Choice To Choose Life:** (Deuteronomy 30:19) What actions do you need to take in order to choose life in this situation?

4. **Jot Down One of The Selected Scriptures That You Feel Led To Mediate On or You Can Use Another Bible Verse That Speaks To Your Situation**
   _____
   _____
   _____

5. **Meditate On Your Selected Scripture and Think About What God Is Saying To You Personally By Way Of This Scripture:**

6. **Declare:** *I am* (say your name) and then say your bible scripture out loud.

7. **Journal Space ...** ✍
   Following is your journal space. You can write down your thoughts, feelings, insights, prayers or anything else that you feel led to write. You can also write down any questions that you want to explore during your quiet time with God.

Decision Dilemma Worksheet

Should I do this...? Or Should I do that...?

Option #1. *Should I?..........*

_____
_____

                       Pros   Cons

_____   _____
_____   _____
_____   _____

What does the Bible say about it? _____
_____
_____
_____

Option #2. *Should I?..........*

_____
_____

                       Pros   Cons

_____   _____
_____   _____
_____   _____

What does the Bible say about it? _____
_____
_____
_____

My Decision. *I will......*

_____
_____
_____

I am ok with my final decision because...

I know in my spirit that this is the right decision for me because...

If I have any second thoughts or reservations about my decision I will...

Decision Dilemma Worksheet

Should I do this...? Or Should I do that...?

Option #1. *Should I?..........*

_____

_____

Pros	Cons
_____	_____
_____	_____
_____	_____

What does the Bible say about it? _____

_____

_____

_____

Option #2. *Should I?..........*

_____

_____

Pros	Cons
_____	_____
_____	_____
_____	_____

What does the Bible say about it? _____

_____

_____

_____

My Decision. *I will......*

_____

_____

_____

I am ok with my final decision because...

I know in my spirit that this is the right decision for me because...

If I have any second thoughts or reservations about my decision I will...

Decision Dilemma Worksheet

Should I do this...? Or Should I do that...?

Option #1. *Should I?..........*

_____
_____

	Pros	Cons
	_____	_____
	_____	_____
	_____	_____

What does the Bible say about it? _____
_____
_____
_____

Option #2. *Should I?..........*

_____
_____

	Pros	Cons
	_____	_____
	_____	_____
	_____	_____

What does the Bible say about it? _____
_____
_____
_____

My Decision. *I will......*

_____
_____
_____

I am ok with my final decision because...

I know in my spirit that this is the right decision for me because...

If I have any second thoughts or reservations about my decision I will...

Your Check In

✸ Good job!

You made it through 30 days of the soul fast. You've got 10 more days to go.

The mere fact that you took 10 days to begin fasting from self-sabotaging choices is another accomplishment on your journey to a better wellbeing. You've now empowered yourself to change some of the results in your life by way of taking responsibility for your choices. (Deuteronomy 30:19)

1.   Did you fast from self-sabotaging choices for the entire 10-day period or did you skip a day? What was this experience like for you?

2.   Did you write in your journal pages each day? What were you surprised to find yourself writing about?

3.   Did you have any insights, discoveries, revelations or breakthroughs during this time?

4.   What do you believe God is saying to you about your choices, now that you've taken 10 days to take a deeper look at your choices in order to detox from self-sabotaging choices?

5.   Are there any other issues that you consider significant to making wise choices that you feel led to continue working on?

The Soul Fast Workbook. Copyright © 2017 by Cassandra Mack.

Section 4
Relationships
Fasting From Toxic People

Fasting From Toxic People

"Shake the dust off your feet"
(Matthew 10:14)

Romans 12: 18 *"If it is possible, as far as it depends on you, live at peace with everyone."*

It's interesting that this Bible verse starts with a very telling clause, *"If it is possible,"* because sometimes in life, especially when you are dealing with a toxic or narcissistic individual it is not always possible to live at peace with everyone or to be okay with how a negative or hateful person is treating you. And sometimes for your own sanity and the wellbeing of your soul; you have to love certain individuals from a safe distance and shake the dust off your feet as you move forward without them in your life.

Even Abraham the father of faith, at some point in his journey, had to distance himself from his nephew Lot in order to walk into his next season of purpose. Abraham loved Lot very much but in order to preserve his peace and move forward in the vision that God gave him for his life, he had to distance himself from Lot, but he did it with no hard feelings and without the bitterness.

Genesis 13: 8 - 9 *"So Abram said to Lot, "Please let there be no strife between you and me, and between my herdsmen and your herdsmen; for we are brethren. Is not the whole land before you? Please separate from me. If you take the left, then I will go to the right; or, if you go to the right, then I will go to the left."*

So, as you can see from Abraham's example, putting a little distance between you and a person who is toxic to your purpose and destiny or a person whose season in your life has come to an end, doesn't have to be dome with malice and meanness. Fasting or even completely detoxing from people who are toxic to your purpose and peace of mind or who are not destined to walk in agreement with you any longer is not about being unkind or unloving, it's about living at peace as far as it depends on you.

Here's a story about two friends who I'll call Rita and Lynne. Rita and Lynne were childhood friends. They shared special secrets. Saw each other through first kisses, first crushes and first periods. They leaned on one another during the tough times. They attended the same college. Majored in the same subject. And as coincidence would have it, they got married around the same time. Rita and Lynne made a promise to each other that they would always be friends to the end.

Rita got a job at a local newspaper. Lynne worked as a manager for a clothing store in the mall. Rita's career started to quickly take off. She went from writing for the local newspaper to landing a senior editorial job for a major fashion magazine. Rita was traveling all over the world, hobnobbing with celebrities and gaining notoriety as a major player in the fashion magazine world.

But somewhere along the line, things started to change between them. Whenever Rita, and Lynne got together, Lynne criticized Rita about her latest article, told her how bad she looked, and teased her about the twenty pounds she gained. In fact, whenever Lynne saw Rita she had something negative to say. Rita found herself becoming more and more self-conscious and doubtful whenever she was around Lynne. And Lynne was becoming more and more hostile and resentful. When Rita confronted Lynne about her behavior, Lynne told Rita to stop being so sensitive and take it all in stride. Rita dropped the subject and continued her friendship with Lynne. But each time they got together, Rita felt like a piece of her self-esteem was being chipped away.

Far too often we stay in relationships that we have outgrown out of misdirected loyalty. Or we tolerate bad behavior out of the need to prove that we're still the same old person and that nothing has really changed. But people do change. Friends sometimes outgrow each other or take different routes in life. And, sometimes when your life takes a different turn and a friend who knew you way back when is tearing you down or every interaction is filled with put downs, competitiveness, hostility or other negative behaviors, then it might be time to detox from that relationship ...but to do so in the spirit of love.

Our relationships do one of three things. They either: help us grow, keep us right where we are or they bring us down. There's no middle ground here. Most people tend to reject this notion because they find it hard to believe that sometimes the very people who claim to love us or who call themselves our friends, can be the very same people who cannot handle our growth or who simply do not have our best interests in mind. When the people who claim to care about you continually mistreat you, try to bring you down or cause you undue stress and drama, it might be time to ask the question: *Do I need to come out from among them?* (2 Corinthians 6:17)

When you're in the presence of a toxic person, be it: a friend, coworker, classmate, family member or even an abusive spouse, over time it starts to take a toll on your soul (mind, will and emotions) and it can also eat away at your physical health. It's extremely difficult to be strong and courageous (Deuteronomy 31:6), or have life abundantly (John 10:10) or enjoy the good medicine of a joyful heart (Proverbs 17:22) or to be in good health even as your soul prospers (3 John 1:2); when you are engaging with a toxic individual, because every interaction with a toxic person slowly but surely chips away at your health and wellbeing. So, it's not just that toxic people grieve us emotionally; it's also the fact that continuous interaction with a toxic person has the potential to kill, steal and destroy our peace of mind, our dreams, our confidence, self-esteem and wellbeing.

So how do you know if a relationship is toxic? Your spirit, soul and body will tell you. If you were to eat something poisonous, your body would immediately try to get rid of it by throwing up. If you got dust in your eye, your eye would start tearing in order to get rid of the debris. If you are severely stressed about something your hair would start falling

The Soul Fast Workbook. Copyright © 2017 by Cassandra Mack.

out or you'll get a tension headache or your skin will break out. All of these indicators are the body's way of protecting you from whatever is not healthy for you. Our spirit is equally protective of us if not more so. If you are fed poisonous words, your heart and mind would give you indicators that you are not emotionally safe. As a result, you might do one of the following: attack the person back verbally with biting words, get as far away from the person as possible, or shut down emotionally whenever you're around the individual. This is known as our fight, flight or freeze response. So, both our body and our souls come with inner mechanisms to let us know when we're in the presence of poisonous people and when we've had enough of their toxic ways.

Clinically speaking, the emotional side effects of toxic relationships include: depression, stress, anxiety, bitterness, despondency, low self-esteem, inadequacy and over time it crushes our motivation. Jesus wants us to have life and have it more abundantly (John 10:10). So, my question for you as we go through the last 10 days of our fast, is this: Are your relationships allowing you to have life and have it more abundantly or are some of your relationships killing, stealing and destroying your joy, peace of mind, confidence and hopeful outlook?

This section of the *Soul Fast Workbook* will deal with your relationships. For the final 10 days of our *Soul Fast,* you will be detoxing from toxic relationships by becoming more mindful of unhealthy relationship behaviors, putting personal boundaries in place and becoming more self-aware of your own behavior in relationships. And remember the greatest love that you can ever experience is the love of God, so don't let fear of upsetting or losing a toxic individual, cause you to tolerate behavior that is not conducive to the wellbeing of your soul, just to be accepted by someone who is clearly showing you that they are unwilling or unable to treat you with care, consideration, respect and kindness. Let's get started on our fourth and final section of *The Soul Fast Workbook.*

Here Are Some Selected Bible Scriptures
That You Can Feast On As You Fast From Toxic People

Genesis 13: 8-9: So Abram said to Lot, "Let's not have any quarreling between you and me, or between your herders and mine, for we are close relatives. 9 Is not the whole land before you? Let's part company. If you go to the left, I'll go to the right; if you go to the right, I'll go to the left."

Matthew 10:13 If the home is worthy, let your peace rest on it; if it is not, let your peace return to you.

Matthew 10:14 If anyone will not welcome you or listen to your words, leave that home or town and shake the dust off your feet.

Matthew 7: 12 Therefore all things whatsoever ye would that men should do to you, do ye even so to them: for this is the law and the prophets.

2 Corinthians 6:14 Do not be yoked together with unbelievers. For what do righteousness and wickedness have in common? Or what fellowship can light have with darkness?

Proverbs 18: 24 One who has unreliable friends soon comes to ruin, but there is a friend who sticks closer than a brother.

Ecclesiastes 4: 9 - 10 Two are better than one; because they have a good reward for their labour. For if they fall, the one will lift up his fellow: but woe to him that is alone when he falleth; for he hath not another to help him up.

Ecclesiastes 4: 12 And if one prevails against him, two shall withstand him; and a threefold cord is not quickly broken.

Matthew 18:19 Again I say unto you, that if two of you shall agree on earth concerning anything that they shall ask, it shall be done for them of my Father who is in heaven.

Amos 3:3 Do two walk together, unless they have agreed to meet?

Matthew 6:33 But seek first the kingdom of God and his righteousness, and all these things will be added to you.

Proverbs 6:28 Can one go upon hot coals, and his feet not be burned?

John 7:24 "Do not judge according to appearance, but judge with righteous judgment."

Proverbs 27:17 As iron sharpens iron, so one person sharpens another.

1 Thessalonians 5:11 Therefore encourage one another and build each other up, just as in fact you are doing.

Hebrews 10:24-25 And let us consider how to stir up one another to love and good works, not neglecting to meet together, as is the habit of some, but encouraging one another, and all the more as you see the Day drawing near.

Ephesians 4:32 Be kind and compassionate to one another, forgiving each other, just as in Christ God forgave you.

Matthew 6:14 For if you forgive other people when they sin against you, your heavenly Father will also forgive you.

Colossians 3:13 Bear with each other and forgive one another if any of you has a grievance against someone. Forgive as the Lord forgave you.

Luke 6:42 How can you say to your brother, 'Brother, let me take the speck out of your eye,' when you yourself fail to see the plank in your own eye? You hypocrite, first take the plank out of your eye, and then you will see clearly to remove the speck from your brother's eye.

1 John 4:1 Dear friends, do not believe every spirit, but test the spirits to see whether they are from God, because many false prophets have gone out into the world.

1 Samuel 18:1 - And it came to pass, when he had made an end of speaking unto Saul, that the soul of Jonathan was knit with the soul of David, and Jonathan loved him as his own soul.

James 2:1-4, My brothers and sisters, believers in our glorious Lord Jesus Christ must not show favoritism. Suppose a man comes into your meeting wearing a gold ring and fine clothes, and a poor man in filthy old clothes also comes in. If you show special attention to the man wearing fine clothes and say, "Here's a good seat for you," but say to the poor man, "You stand there" or "Sit on the floor by my feet," have you not discriminated among yourselves and become judges with evil thoughts?

1 Corinthians 15:33: Don't be fooled by people who say such things, for "bad company corrupts good character."

1 Samuel 24:17 He said to David, "You are more righteous than I; for you have dealt well with me, while I have dealt wickedly with you.

Matthew 5:44 But I say to you, love your enemies, and pray for those who persecute you

1 Corinthians 16:14 Do everything in love.

Day 31

✸Today's Date: _____

Worksheet for Day 31

Fasting From Toxic People

1. **Pray:** Start your day with prayer. Thank and praise God for all of your blessings including the blessing of another day of life. Talk to God about whatever is on your heart and mind. Pray for the clarity and courage to deal with the people in your life that you might need to either: love from a distance, restructure the relationship so that it does not bring you out of integrity and wellbeing or whom you might have to have a difficult but necessary conversation with because the relationship is becoming toxic or it's undermining your purpose and progress.

2. **Identify A Relationship That You Believe Is Toxic:**
I believe my relationship with _____ is toxic. I believe this because
_____
I need to take a fast from this relationship because _____
_____
_____
_____
This is how this relationship is affecting me. Mentally, whenever I think of this person or whenever I'm in their presence I notice that I tend to _____
_____
_____
Emotionally, when I am around this person I feel _____
_____
_____
Spiritually, when I am around this person, my spirit feels _____
_____
_____
It's affecting my physically by making me feel _____
_____
_____

3. **Ask God: Does This Relationship Produce Good Fruit or Is It Creating Undue Stress, Taking Me Off My Path & Bringing Out The Worst In Me?**

4. **Ask God: Should You Come Out From Among Them?** (2 Corinthians 6:17)
What actions do you need to take in order to come out from among them?

5. Jot Down One of The Selected Scriptures That You Feel Led To Mediate On or You Can Use Another Bible Verse That Speaks To Your Situation

_____

_____

_____

6. Meditate On Your Selected Scripture and Think About What God Is Saying To You Personally By Way Of This Scripture:

7. Declare: Say your bible scripture out loud.

8. Journal Space ... ✍

This is your journal space. You can write down your thoughts, feelings, insights, prayers or anything else that you feel led to write. You can also write down any questions that you want to explore during your quiet time with God.

✍ _____

_____

_____

_____

_____

_____

_____

_____

_____

_____

_____

_____

_____

_____

_____

_____

_____

_____

_____

_____

_____

Day 32

✸Today's Date: _____

Worksheet for Day 32

Fasting From Toxic People

1. **Pray:** Start your day with prayer. Thank and praise God for all of your blessings including the blessing of another day of life. Talk to God about whatever is on your heart and mind. Pray for the clarity and courage to deal with the people in your life that you might need to either: love from a distance, restructure the relationship so that it does not bring you out of integrity and wellbeing or whom you might have to have a difficult but necessary conversation with because the relationship is becoming toxic or it's undermining your purpose and progress.

2. **Identify A Relationship That You Believe Is Toxic:**
I believe my relationship with _____ is toxic. I believe this because
_____
I need to fast from this relationship because _____
_____
_____
_____
This is how this relationship is affecting me. Mentally, whenever I think of this person or whenever I'm in their presence I notice that I tend to _____
_____
_____
Emotionally, when I am around this person I feel _____
_____
_____
Spiritually, when I am around this person, my spirit feels _____
_____
_____
It's affecting my physically by making me feel _____
_____
_____

3. **Ask God: Does This Relationship Produce Good Fruit or Is It Creating Undue Stress, Taking Me Off My Path & Bringing Out The Worst In Me?**

4. **Ask God: Should You Come Out From Among Them?** (2 Corinthians 6:17)
What actions do you need to take in order to come out from among them?

5. **Jot Down One of The Selected Scriptures That You Feel Led To Mediate On or You Can Use Another Bible Verse That Speaks To Your Situation**

The Soul Fast Workbook. Copyright © 2017 by Cassandra Mack.

_____

_____

_____

6. Meditate On Your Selected Scripture and Think About What God Is Saying To You Personally By Way Of This Scripture:

7. Declare: Say your bible scripture out loud.

8. Journal Space ... ✍

This is your journal space. You can write down your thoughts, feelings, insights, prayers or anything else that you feel led to write. You can also write down any questions that you want to explore during your quiet time with God.

✍ _____

_____

_____

_____

_____

_____

_____

_____

_____

_____

_____

_____

_____

_____

_____

_____

_____

_____

_____

_____

_____

_____

Day 33

*Today's Date: _____

Worseet for Day 33

(Worksheet for Day 33)

Fasting From Toxic People

1. **Pray:** Start your day with prayer. Thank and praise God for all of your blessings including the blessing of another day of life. Talk to God about whatever is on your heart and mind. Pray for the clarity and courage to deal with the people in your life that you might need to either: love from a distance, restructure the relationship so that it does not bring you out of integrity and wellbeing or whom you might have to have a difficult but necessary conversation with because the relationship is becoming toxic or it's undermining your purpose and progress.

2. **Identify A Relationship That You Believe Is Toxic:**
I believe my relationship with _____ is toxic. I believe this because
_____
I need to fast from this relationship because _____
_____
_____
_____
This is how this relationship is affecting me. Mentally, whenever I think of this person or whenever I'm in their presence I notice that I tend to _____
_____
_____
Emotionally, when I am around this person I feel _____
_____
_____
Spiritually, when I am around this person, my spirit feels _____
_____
_____
It's affecting my physically by making me feel _____
_____
_____

3. **Ask God: Does This Relationship Produce Good Fruit or Is It Creating Undue Stress, Taking Me Off My Path & Bringing Out The Worst In Me?**

4. **Ask God: Should You Come Out From Among Them?** (2 Corinthians 6:17)
What actions do you need to take in order to come out from among them?

5. Jot Down One of The Selected Scriptures That You Feel Led To Mediate On or You Can Use Another Bible Verse That Speaks To Your Situation

_____

_____

_____

6. Meditate On Your Selected Scripture and Think About What God Is Saying To You Personally By Way Of This Scripture:

7. Declare: Say your bible scripture out loud.

8. Journal Space ... ✍

This is your journal space. You can write down your thoughts, feelings, insights, prayers or anything else that you feel led to write. You can also write down any questions that you want to explore during your quiet time with God.

✍ _____

_____

_____

_____

_____

_____

_____

_____

_____

_____

_____

_____

_____

_____

_____

_____

_____

_____

_____

_____

_____

_____

Day 34

❋Today's Date: _____

Worksheet for Day 34

Fasting From Toxic People

1. **Pray:** Start your day with prayer. Thank and praise God for all of your blessings including the blessing of another day of life. Talk to God about whatever is on your heart and mind. Pray for the clarity and courage to deal with the people in your life that you might need to either: love from a distance, restructure the relationship so that it does not bring you out of integrity and wellbeing or whom you might have to have a difficult but necessary conversation with because the relationship is becoming toxic or it's undermining your purpose and progress.

2. **Identify A Relationship That You Believe Is Toxic:**
I believe my relationship with _____ is toxic. I believe this because
_____
I need to fast from this relationship because _____
_____
_____
_____
This is how this relationship is affecting me. Mentally, whenever I think of this person or whenever I'm in their presence I notice that I tend to _____
_____
_____
Emotionally, when I am around this person I feel _____
_____
_____
Spiritually, when I am around this person, my spirit feels _____
_____
_____
It's affecting my physically by making me feel _____
_____
_____

3. **Ask God: Does This Relationship Produce Good Fruit or Is It Creating Undue Stress, Taking Me Off My Path & Bringing Out The Worst In Me?**

4. **Ask God: Should You Come Out From Among Them?** (2 Corinthians 6:17)
What actions do you need to take in order to come out from among them?

The Soul Fast Workbook. Copyright © 2017 by Cassandra Mack.

5. Jot Down One of The Selected Scriptures That You Feel Led To Mediate On or You Can Use Another Bible Verse That Speaks To Your Situation

_____

_____

_____

6. Meditate On Your Selected Scripture and Think About What God Is Saying To You Personally By Way Of This Scripture:

7. Declare: Say your bible scripture out loud.

8. Journal Space ... ✍

This is your journal space. You can write down your thoughts, feelings, insights, prayers or anything else that you feel led to write. You can also write down any questions that you want to explore during your quiet time with God.

✍ _____

_____

_____

_____

_____

_____

_____

_____

_____

_____

_____

_____

_____

_____

_____

_____

_____

_____

_____

_____

_____

_____

Day 35

✸ Today's Date: _____

Worksheet for Day 35

Fasting From Toxic People

1. **Pray:** Start your day with prayer. Thank and praise God for all of your blessings including the blessing of another day of life. Talk to God about whatever is on your heart and mind. Pray for the clarity and courage to deal with the people in your life that you might need to either: love from a distance, restructure the relationship so that it does not bring you out of integrity and wellbeing or whom you might have to have a difficult but necessary conversation with because the relationship is becoming toxic or it's undermining your purpose and progress.

2. **Identify A Relationship That You Believe Is Toxic:**
I believe my relationship with _____ is toxic. I believe this because _____
I need to fast from this relationship because _____
_____
_____
_____
This is how this relationship is affecting me. Mentally, whenever I think of this person or whenever I'm in their presence I notice that I tend to _____
_____
Emotionally, when I am around this person I feel _____
_____
Spiritually, when I am around this person, my spirit feels _____
_____
It's affecting my physically by making me feel _____
_____
_____

3. **Ask God: Does This Relationship Produce Good Fruit or Is It Creating Undue Stress, Taking Me Off My Path & Bringing Out The Worst In Me?**

4. **Ask God: Should You Come Out From Among Them?** (2 Corinthians 6:17)
What actions do you need to take in order to come out from among them?

5. Jot Down One of The Selected Scriptures That You Feel Led To Mediate On or You Can Use Another Bible Verse That Speaks To Your Situation

_____

_____

_____

6. Meditate On Your Selected Scripture and Think About What God Is Saying To You Personally By Way Of This Scripture:

7. Declare: Say your bible scripture out loud.

8. Journal Space ... ✎

This is your journal space. You can write down your thoughts, feelings, insights, prayers or anything else that you feel led to write. You can also write down any questions that you want to explore during your quiet time with God.

✎ _____

_____

_____

_____

_____

_____

_____

_____

_____

_____

_____

_____

_____

_____

_____

_____

_____

_____

_____

_____

_____

Wonder Twin Powers Activate

The Power Of Getting Into Agreement With The Right People

When I was a kid, one of my favorite things to do on Saturday mornings was to get a big bowl of Peanut Butter Captain Crunch cereal and watch Saturday morning cartoons.

I grew up in the age where TV's actually went off the air for a few hours each night. Somewhere around 2am the announcer would come on the air and say... "We now conclude our broadcast day." Then the National Anthem came on, and then there was a loud continual beeeeeeeeeeeeeep until the TV went static. Anybody remember this? If so, you are officially an old school head like me.

Well back in the day, one of my favorite cartoons was the "Wonder Twins." For those of you who don't know about the Wonder Twins, let me break it down for you. The Wonder Twins, Zan and Jayna, were an extraterrestrial twin brother and sister superhero duo who were part of the animated Hanna-Barbera television series Super Friends. They subsequently appeared in comics based on the animated series, and were later introduced into the DC Comics and even made an appearance on the TV series "Smallville."

What's so fascinating about the Wonder Twins is that their full power could only be activated when they came into agreement and touched each other and then declared the Right Words... *"Wonder Twin powers activate!"*

Ironically, speaking the right words aloud or Declaring was just as important to the activation process as the two of them gathering together to come into agreement.

Not only that, if one was of reach from the other, they were unable to activate the full measure of their powers, because their power was in their coming together in agreement. What's even more interesting about these two powerful people is that before they could be transformed, so to speak, they each had to speak life into the thing they wanted to be by saying something along the lines of... "Shape of a tree...", "Form of water..."

Isn't it ironic, that nothing happens, that nothing takes form, that nothing manifests and materializes, THAT NOTHING COMES INTO EXISTENCE even in the world of animation and imagination. UNTIL IT IS SPOKEN, AGREED UPON and DECREED?

Now Zan the brother was able to transform into water in any form be it solid, liquid, or gas. Plus, he had the power to increase in mass by flowing into any BODY OF WATER that was within his DOMAIN. Whereas, Jayna was able to transform herself into any animal that she chose; be it a swimming one, a creeping thing or any foul of the air

Now here's where it gets deep, since Jayna had to be able to vocalize her intended form that she wants to transform herself into beforehand, she had to know the right name of the animal or the right words to speak before she could call those things that be not as though they were. In other words, she has to have the ENOUGH WORD inside of her so that the WORD naturally and instinctively flowed out of her, thus manifesting the life affirming and creative power of the SPOKEN WORD. In fact, saying the wrong words could cause her to speak the wrong thing into existence subsequently causing her to take on the WRONG IDENTITY, thus reducing her power to stand strong against the schemes of the enemy.

So, for example if she needed to be transformed into a Lion in order to defeat a Hyena but viewed herself as a grasshopper in her own sight and as a result called herself a GRASSHOPPER, then by nature of the power of her own tongue she would then reduce herself to a mere GRASSHOPPER and feel inadequate in her own sight whenever life required her to have courage like a Lion so she could defeat the hyenas of life.

Can you imagine a mere Grasshopper trying to defeat a Hyena, especially knowing that Hyenas are ravenous creatures that travel in packs? The Hyena himself would laugh hysterically, because he would clearly be able to see by Jayna's own self-prophesy that she was showing up to a dog fight (where things get dirty) as a mere grasshopper when she has the power to be a lion.

So, if Jayna wanted to walk in the fullness of her authority as a Wonder Twin and defeat whatever enemies come against her, she must recognize that the power to defeat whatever is trying to come against her...is in her words and in who she gets in agreement with. Feel me?

What I am saying by way of the *Wonder Twins* cartoon is simply this: Where can it be said, that just like the character Jayna in the Wonder Twins, that you have to speak your faith into existence beforehand so that you can transform who you are mentally and emotionally in order to get the victory?

Where can it be said that just like the Wonder Twins you've got to get in agreement with The Creator, the right people and the right ministry so that you can get enough WORD IN YOU to be transformed and activate your abundant life?

Here's the other piece of it: If we know that in the beginning was the WORD, then wouldn't it make sense to get as much WORD in you as possible, so that you can begin and end anything you set your mind to from a place of revelation, power and strength.

And when it comes to activating our touch and agree powers: Matthew 18: 19 -20 tells us this.... "*Again, I say to you, that if two of you agree on earth about anything that they*

The Soul Fast Workbook. Copyright © 2017 by Cassandra Mack.

may ask, it shall be done for them by My Father who is in heaven. For where two or three have gathered together in My name, I am there in their midst."

So today, know that if a fictional cartoon character has enough sense to get into agreement with the right people and step away from those who are trying to come against her ....then surely you and I as intelligent, powerful, fearfully and wonderfully made children of the Almighty God can activate our power, love and sound mind to come out from among the toxic people in our lives so that we can get connected to people who want to walk with us in shared faith, shared purpose and shared destiny and develop relationships that bear good fruit.

Day 36

Worksheet for Day 36

Fasting From Toxic People

1. **Pray:** Start your day with prayer. Thank and praise God for all of your blessings including the blessing of another day of life. Talk to God about whatever is on your heart and mind. Pray for the clarity and courage to deal with the people in your life that you might need to either: love from a distance, restructure the relationship so that it does not bring you out of integrity and wellbeing or whom you might have to have a difficult but necessary conversation with because the relationship is becoming toxic or it's undermining your purpose and progress.

2. **Identify A Relationship That You Believe Is Toxic:**
I believe my relationship with _____ is toxic. I believe this because
_____
I need to fast from this relationship because _____
_____
_____
_____
This is how this relationship is affecting me. Mentally, whenever I think of this person or whenever I'm in their presence I notice that I tend to _____
_____
_____
Emotionally, when I am around this person I feel _____
_____
Spiritually, when I am around this person, my spirit feels _____
_____
It's affecting my physically by making me feel _____
_____
_____

3. **Ask God: Does This Relationship Produce Good Fruit or Is It Creating Undue Stress, Taking Me Off My Path & Bringing Out The Worst In Me?**

4. **Ask God: Should You Come Out From Among Them?** (2 Corinthians 6:17) What actions do you need to take in order to come out from among them?

5. **Jot Down One of The Selected Scriptures That You Feel Led To Mediate On or You Can Use Another Bible Verse That Speaks To Your Situation**

_____
_____
_____

6. Meditate On Your Selected Scripture and Think About What God Is Saying To You Personally By Way Of This Scripture:

7. Declare: Say your bible scripture out loud.

8. Journal Space ... ✍

This is your journal space. You can write down your thoughts, feelings, insights, prayers or anything else that you feel led to write. You can also write down any questions that you want to explore during your quiet time with God.

✍ _____

_____
_____
_____
_____
_____
_____
_____
_____
_____
_____
_____
_____
_____
_____
_____
_____
_____
_____
_____
_____
_____

Day 37

Worksheet for Day 37

Fasting From Toxic People

1. **Pray:** Start your day with prayer. Thank and praise God for all of your blessings including the blessing of another day of life. Talk to God about whatever is on your heart and mind. Pray for the clarity and courage to deal with the people in your life that you might need to either: love from a distance, restructure the relationship so that it does not bring you out of integrity and wellbeing or whom you might have to have a difficult but necessary conversation with because the relationship is becoming toxic or it's undermining your purpose and progress.

2. **Identify A Relationship That You Believe Is Toxic:**
I believe my relationship with _____ is toxic. I believe this because
_____
I need to fast from this relationship because _____
_____
_____
_____
This is how this relationship is affecting me. Mentally, whenever I think of this person or whenever I'm in their presence I notice that I tend to _____
_____
_____
Emotionally, when I am around this person I feel _____
_____
Spiritually, when I am around this person, my spirit feels _____
_____
It's affecting my physically by making me feel _____
_____
_____

3. **Ask God: Does This Relationship Produce Good Fruit or Is It Creating Undue Stress, Taking Me Off My Path & Bringing Out The Worst In Me?**

4. **Ask God: Should You Come Out From Among Them?** (2 Corinthians 6:17)
What actions do you need to take in order to come out from among them?

5. Jot Down One of The Selected Scriptures That You Feel Led To Mediate On or You Can Use Another Bible Verse That Speaks To Your Situation

_____

_____

_____

6. Meditate On Your Selected Scripture and Think About What God Is Saying To You Personally By Way Of This Scripture:

7. Declare: Say your bible scripture out loud.

8. Journal Space ... ✍

This is your journal space. You can write down your thoughts, feelings, insights, prayers or anything else that you feel led to write. You can also write down any questions that you want to explore during your quiet time with God.

✍ _____

_____

_____

_____

_____

_____

_____

_____

_____

_____

_____

_____

_____

_____

_____

_____

_____

_____

_____

_____

_____

_____

Day 38

✹Today's Date: _____

Worksheet for Day 38

Fasting From Toxic People

1. **Pray:** Start your day with prayer. Thank and praise God for all of your blessings including the blessing of another day of life. Talk to God about whatever is on your heart and mind. Pray for the clarity and courage to deal with the people in your life that you might need to either: love from a distance, restructure the relationship so that it does not bring you out of integrity and wellbeing or whom you might have to have a difficult but necessary conversation with because the relationship is becoming toxic or it's undermining your purpose and progress.

2. **Identify A Relationship That You Believe Is Toxic:**
I believe my relationship with _____ is toxic. I believe this because
_____
I need to fast from this relationship because _____
_____
_____
_____
This is how this relationship is affecting me. Mentally, whenever I think of this person or whenever I'm in their presence I notice that I tend to _____
_____
_____
Emotionally, when I am around this person I feel _____
_____
_____
Spiritually, when I am around this person, my spirit feels _____
_____
_____
It's affecting my physically by making me feel _____
_____
_____

3. **Ask God: Does This Relationship Produce Good Fruit or Is It Creating Undue Stress, Taking Me Off My Path & Bringing Out The Worst In Me?**

4. **Ask God: Should You Come Out From Among Them?** (2 Corinthians 6:17)
What actions do you need to take in order to come out from among them?

5. Jot Down One of The Selected Scriptures That You Feel Led To Mediate On or You Can Use Another Bible Verse That Speaks To Your Situation

_____

_____

_____

6. Meditate On Your Selected Scripture and Think About What God Is Saying To You Personally By Way Of This Scripture:

7. Declare: Say your bible scripture out loud.

8. Journal Space ... ✍

This is your journal space. You can write down your thoughts, feelings, insights, prayers or anything else that you feel led to write. You can also write down any questions that you want to explore during your quiet time with God.

✍ _____

_____

_____

_____

_____

_____

_____

_____

_____

_____

_____

_____

_____

_____

_____

_____

_____

_____

_____

_____

_____

Day 39

✹Today's Date: ____________________

Worksheet for Day 39

Fasting From Toxic People

1. **Pray:** Start your day with prayer. Thank and praise God for all of your blessings including the blessing of another day of life. Talk to God about whatever is on your heart and mind. Pray for the clarity and courage to deal with the people in your life that you might need to either: love from a distance, restructure the relationship so that it does not bring you out of integrity and wellbeing or whom you might have to have a difficult but necessary conversation with because the relationship is becoming toxic or it's undermining your purpose and progress.

2. **Identify A Relationship That You Believe Is Toxic:**
I believe my relationship with ____________________ is toxic. I believe this because ____________________

I need to fast from this relationship because ____________________
____
____
____

This is how this relationship is affecting me. Mentally, whenever I think of this person or whenever I'm in their presence I notice that I tend to ____________________
____
____

Emotionally, when I am around this person I feel ____________________
____
____

Spiritually, when I am around this person, my spirit feels ____________________
____
____

It's affecting my physically by making me feel ____________________
____
____

3. **Ask God: Does This Relationship Produce Good Fruit or Is It Creating Undue Stress, Taking Me Off My Path & Bringing Out The Worst In Me?**

4. **Ask God: Should You Come Out From Among Them?** (2 Corinthians 6:17) What actions do you need to take in order to come out from among them?

5. Jot Down One of The Selected Scriptures That You Feel Led To Mediate On or You Can Use Another Bible Verse That Speaks To Your Situation

_____

_____

_____

6. Meditate On Your Selected Scripture and Think About What God Is Saying To You Personally By Way Of This Scripture:

7. Declare: Say your bible scripture out loud.

8. Journal Space ... ✍

This is your journal space. You can write down your thoughts, feelings, insights, prayers or anything else that you feel led to write. You can also write down any questions that you want to explore during your quiet time with God.

✍ _____

_____

_____

_____

_____

_____

_____

_____

_____

_____

_____

_____

_____

_____

_____

_____

_____

_____

_____

_____

_____

_____

Day 40

✹ Today's Date: _____

Worksheet for Day 40

Fasting From Toxic People

1. **Pray:** Start your day with prayer. Thank and praise God for all of your blessings including the blessing of another day of life. Talk to God about whatever is on your heart and mind. Pray for the clarity and courage to deal with the people in your life that you might need to either: love from a distance, restructure the relationship so that it does not bring you out of integrity and wellbeing or whom you might have to have a difficult but necessary conversation with because the relationship is becoming toxic or it's undermining your purpose and progress.

2. **Identify A Relationship That You Believe Is Toxic:**
I believe my relationship with _____ is toxic. I believe this because _____

I need to fast from this relationship because _____
_____
_____
_____

This is how this relationship is affecting me. Mentally, whenever I think of this person or whenever I'm in their presence I notice that I tend to _____
_____

Emotionally, when I am around this person I feel _____
_____

Spiritually, when I am around this person, my spirit feels _____
_____

It's affecting my physically by making me feel _____
_____
_____

3. **Ask God: Does This Relationship Produce Good Fruit or Is It Creating Undue Stress, Taking Me Off My Path & Bringing Out The Worst In Me?**

4. **Ask God: Should You Come Out From Among Them?** (2 Corinthians 6:17)
What actions do you need to take in order to come out from among them?

5. Jot Down One of The Selected Scriptures That You Feel Led To Mediate On or You Can Use Another Bible Verse That Speaks To Your Situation

_____

_____

_____

6. Meditate On Your Selected Scripture and Think About What God Is Saying To You Personally By Way Of This Scripture:

7. Declare: Say your bible scripture out loud.

8. Journal Space ... ✍

This is your journal space. You can write down your thoughts, feelings, insights, prayers or anything else that you feel led to write. You can also write down any questions that you want to explore during your quiet time with God.

✍ _____

_____

_____

_____

_____

_____

_____

_____

_____

_____

_____

_____

_____

_____

_____

_____

_____

_____

_____

_____

_____

_____

_____

Your Check In

Congratulations. You did it! You completed the soul fast. I am so proud of you.

Take a moment to celebrate your completion of your personal Soul Fast. You are stronger, better and wiser because of it.

Give God the glory for enabling you to go on this journey and successfully complete it.

1. Did you fast from toxic people for the entire 10-day period or did you skip a day? What was this experience like for you?

2. Did you write in your journal pages each day? What were you surprised to find yourself writing about?

3. Did you have any insights, discoveries, revelations or breakthroughs during this time?

4. What do you believe God is saying to you about some of your relationships now that you've completed the entire fast?

5. Even though our Soul Fast is completed, are there any other relationship issues that you feel led to continue working on? What are you going to do moving forward?

My Closing Words to You

Congratulations! You did it. You've completed *The Soul Fast*. Thank you for giving me the privilege of guiding you through your 40-day journey to better spiritual, mental and emotional wellbeing. My prayer for you is that you experience God in a deeper way and experience more of God's love, grace, presence, power and provision.

I believe that by completing this soul fast you have positioned yourself to be more receptive to greater blessings and bigger breakthroughs. I pray that any fruitlessness you experienced in the past will be replaced by promotion and fruitfulness. I pray that any areas where your soul has been broken or made heavy will be restored and made whole. I call forth healing for your mind and your emotions. I call forth your anointing to manifest clearly in your life so that you may be fruitful in your endeavors and multiply everything that our Creator has blessed you with. I speak clarity into your life; confusion shall not have any power over your mind. I call forth divine wisdom in your life so that you can make wise decisions and enjoy the fruit of wise choices. I declare by faith that God will supply all of your needs – spiritually, mentally, emotionally, physically and financially. Thank you Lord in advance for hearing this prayer. I pray these things in Jesus name. Amen!

Start declaring God's promises which are all found in the Bible, over your life and if you are a parent speak them over your children. Prayer is the oxygen of our spirit and the elixir to the soul.

Now that you have experienced the good fruit of prayer, try to devote a few minutes each morning for prayer and bible reading. 15 focused minutes each morning can make all the difference in the world. Even 5 minutes of focused prayer renews the mind and fuels the spirit with the power to stand and with the power to get back up over and over again every time we fall. If you'd like to continue your growth, stop by my Online Bookstore at: **StrategiesForEmpoweredLiving.com** and check out our resources and programs designed to help you unlock your potential and seize your success.

I wish you every good thing that your heart desires. Be blessed and prosper.

To your success,
Cassandra Mack

The Soul Fast Workbook. Copyright © 2017 by Cassandra Mack.

Bring Cassandra Mack's Soul Fast Workshop to Your Women's Group or Church

THE SOUL FAST
worshop for women

Because Sometimes In Order To Have Life Abundantly
You Have To Address What's Eating You

A BIBLE-BASED WORKSHOP FOR

WOMEN'S GROUPS

- Identify mindsets, beliefs and habits that bring you down and weigh on your spirit.
- Identify the stressful relationships in your life and protect your spirit from the harmful effects of negativity and toxic people.
- Guard your heart against unhealthy emotional attachments that play with your mind, break you down as a woman, and try to make you believe that you are un worthy and not redeemed.
- Shut the door on unhealthy soul ties that seek to devour your soul and tie you up in deception, drama, and despair.
- Refuse to settle for any mindset, situation or relationship that pulls you away from purpose and destiny.

BOOK CHRISTIAN LIFE COACH CASSANDRA MACK TODAY!

Cassandra Mack, MSW is a highly sought-after empowerment specialist, author, executive life coach and master facilitator who addresses critical issues affecting human development. With a background in social work, human behavior and youth development, leadership mentoring and training and capacity building, Cassandra Mack bridges the clinical with the biblical to translate powerful Kingdom principles into practical tools for personal empowerment that individuals and organizations can use to transform their lives and create a personal roadmap for success.

BOOK YOUR GROUP WORKSHOP TODAY
KingdomKeyswithCassandraMack.com

The Soul Fast Workbook. Copyright © 2017 by Cassandra Mack.
P. 145

The Soul Fast Workbook. Copyright © 2017 by Cassandra Mack.

Food for Your Soul

Bonus Inspirational Writings by Cassandra Mack

The Soul Fast Workbook. Copyright © 2017 by Cassandra Mack.

What An Expired Quart of Milk Taught Me About God's Provision & Right On Time Blessings

By: Cassandra Mack

The date was February 24, 2015. I was rushing out of the house to take my son to school and set up for a presentation that I had to make. We were already about 15 minutes behind schedule, so the breakfast of choice for my son was a bowl of Cheerios with two slices of whole wheat toast. However, when I looked in the bread box, I noticed that we were out of bread, so I figured a bowl of Cheerios with milk would have to suffice.

As I was sending out a last-minute email my son got the milk from the fridge so he could pour it into his cereal. Since I don't drink milk but buy it exclusively for my son and he pays attention to detail, he noticed that the expiration date on the carton was February 24, 2015. And since I did not have time to prepare breakfast or stop at the neighborhood deli to get bagels without making him late for school and missing my bus....it looked like we were in a bit of a pickle. At least that's how things appeared in the natural.

I didn't want to send my son to school on an empty stomach but I could not afford to be late for this very important presentation, so I told him the best he could do on this particular morning was to grab a handful of dry Cheerios and tough it out until lunch time. That's when my son carefully examined the milk cartoon and said...” Ma, let me smell the milk to see if it's still good.” I said okay.

He smelled it and then said, *“It smells alright but just to make sure, let me pour a little bit in a cup and taste it to make sure it's not spoiled.”* Since I am lactose intolerant I had to trust my son's judgment. And guess what? Although the date on the milk read February 9th and the day that this incident happened was on February 24, nearly two weeks past the last sale date, believe it or not, the milk was still good.

Isn't it funny, how a blessing can come to you in the most unexpected way? Now let me be clear here, one thing I am not is naive, so I clearly recognize that for some people being able to make use of milk that is almost two weeks past the expiration date may not seem like that big of a deal. I get it. Trust me I do. But since I needed to get out of the house quickly on this particular morning, and I did not have anything else that I could quickly throw together for my son to eat and still get him to school on time as well as get to my presentation on time, that quart of still-good milk meant the world to me. And as soon as my son confirmed that the milk was still good, I smiled because I recognized the milk for what it was.... a Right On-Time Blessing.

Always remember to appreciate every little blessing that comes your way. And wherever you are in your life, be thankful for God's provision...even if the only provision you have at the moment is enough gas to get to work today or enough food in your fridge to make a pot of beans or a PB & J sandwich. No matter how seemingly small the blessing, when a blessing comes your way, acknowledge it, appreciate it and most of all thank God for it. Today open up your eyes of appreciation and look for the blessings that are already present in your life.

David Danced, Moses Went To The Mountain Top & Abraham Laid It All On The Altar: What Are You Going to Do to Get Your Breakthrough?

There are times in our lives when nothing we do seems to work or stick. You upgrade your wardrobe, change your surroundings, get a new job, change the way you talk, change the company you keep, but still can't get your breakthrough. You join the gym. Sign up for a new seminar. Read a new book. As a result, you start to get closer to the thing that you are seeking, but you are still not close enough for a major breakthrough. Have you ever thought about why this is happening?

Perhaps just maybe since you have already tried everything else, it might be time to go deeper in God. To go deeper in your prayer life, deeper in your devotional time, deeper in reading God's word...so that you can breakthrough and step into your season of success.

Matthew 7:7 gives us God's formula for a major breakthrough. This scripture tells us to do 3 things, to ASK, SEEK and KNOCK... "Ask, and it shall be given unto you; seek, and ye shall find; knock, and it shall be opened unto you. So, there is a 3-part process to breakthrough to your season of success. And as long as what we are seeking lines up with God's plan for our lives, the formula works. It's just a matter of God's perfect timing.

Many people take this scripture in Matthew 7:7 to mean, ask without doing anything in return and you will receive your heart's desires. But the law of reciprocity is clear, you have to sow into a thing if you are to reap a full harvest from it. After we ask we have to also seek and knock. We have to make sure that what we are asking for aligns with God's word and His will. Then we need to exercise the necessary patience to wait for it, because everything happens in God's perfect timing.

With this in mind, what are you going to do to get your breakthrough? In the bible, we see that David danced, Moses went up to the Mountain top and Abraham laid it all on the altar; but what will you do to get your breakthrough?

Let's look at how the 3 aforementioned individuals, asked, sought and knocked. We'll start with David. David was a man after God's own heart. He worshiped God like no other in song, prayer, praise and dance. He wrote quite a few of the Psalms. David wasn't perfect. In many ways, he was a hot mess. He coveted another man's wife, Bathsheba, which led him down the path of adultery and murder, but he was wise enough to know that he needed to repent and go deeper in God if he was going to live out God's plan for his life.

As a result of David's actions, the baby that was conceived through his affair with Bathsheba died. After the baby died, David pulled himself together, washed up, put on some lotion and changed his clothes. Then, he went to the Tabernacle and worshiped in prayer, song and danced. To the man who is guided by his intellect rather than his faith, David's actions may seem a bit strange. Why would anyone in their right mind sing and dance after the death of their child? However, as a man of faith David knew that if he was to get his breakthrough, he had to humble himself before the Lord and acknowledge

The Soul Fast Workbook. Copyright © 2017 by Cassandra Mack.

the goodness of God, even in the midst of his personal pain. David's breakthrough came with the birth of his son Solomon, who was considered the wisest man in the world and who later wrote the book of Proverbs.

Let's look at Moses' mountaintop experience. Moses had a special relationship with God. Not only did Moses ask God to reveal his glory, but he sought God and knocked on the door of God's presence like no other. Moses was bold. He talked to God like you would talk to a trusted friend. His relationship with God was personal. So much so that Moses was also bold enough to ask God to show himself to be true. However, God required something of Moses as well. Moses had to come up higher and remove his sandals which is significant of having to remove the things in our lives, that God needs us to remove. Moses had to come up to Mount Sinai and he had to do it alone. He couldn't bring his brother Aaron or his sister Miriam with him. And out of Moses's mountaintop experience came The Ten Commandments. It was noted that when Moses came down from Mount Sinai, his hair was white and he had a supernatural glow. Moses's breakthrough came in the form of a crystal-clear word from God.

Now let's look at Abraham's altar experience. The story goes that God asked Abraham to sacrifice his beloved son Isaac as an offering. Although everything inside of Abraham did not want to do this, he prepared himself to carry out God's request. Of course, God was not going to allow Abraham to sacrifice his son. That was never God's plan. It was a test for Abraham to look within to see if he was willing to let go of the very thing he thought he could not give up and give over to God. This ultimate example of sacrifice is not about promoting sacrificial killing of our kids, but to illustrate that sometimes you've got to be willing to let go of the very thing that you have given birth to and lived with for years, the thing you think you cannot live without - in order to get your breakthrough. Abraham got his breakthrough in the form of o covenant with God to become the father of many nations.

Whatever breakthrough you are seeking, whatever season of life that you are in, whatever you've been hoping for, wishing for and praying for... the question to consider is this: *What are you going to do to get your breakthrough?*

✓ **Are You Going to Dance Like David Did?** - which represents going deeper in your praise and worship.

✓ **Are You Going to Go to The Mountaintop Like Moses Did?** – which represents seeking a close personal relationship with God, talking to God about everything.

✓ **Are You Going to Lay It On The Altar Like Abraham Did?** – which represents your willingness to be obedient and let go of whatever it is that God is asking you to let go of and give over to him.

And since God is no respecter of persons; meaning if He gave these 3 individuals their breakthrough, He will give a breakthrough to you too. Therefore, the only question that remains to be answered as it relates to your breakthrough is this: Will you worship like David, take some time alone in order to have a mountaintop experience like Moses or will you follow Abraham's example of obedience and lay it all on the altar for God?

Always Remember That Little Foxes Grow Up to Become Big Foxes With Insatiable Appetites

By: Cassandra Mack

Ever heard the saying: *"It's the little foxes that spoil the vine?"* Well it's true. The <u>Song of Solomon 2:15</u> warns us about the little foxes. It warns us to…" Catch *for us the foxes, the little foxes that ruin the vineyards, our vineyards that are in bloom."*

The fascinating love story in Solomon's song contains many interesting images. One is of a beautiful vineyard in early spring. The vines, however, are threatened by little foxes that come in to eat the tender grapes before they are ripe. Hence comes the plea to capture or "take" the foxes and prevent them from spoiling the vineyard. One obvious spiritual application is to be aware of the understated danger of what we may think of as "little sins" that can lead us down a path that isn't good for us.

For example, let's say that you have a co-worker who you are sexually attracted to and enjoy spending time with but you're married. So, you rationalize to yourself and figure no harm done if you choose to have lunch together regularly building emotional intimacy. You may think there's no harm done, because you are not sleeping together, but by going out to lunch regularly with someone who you are sexually attracted to and feel emotionally connected to, you open the door for the "little fox" of attraction to spoil the vine of your marriage. And before you know it, you start fantasizing about what it would be like to be intimate with your co-worker. You start sending suggestive texts, your emails get racier and racier. You exchange provocative photos. And before you know it what started out as a "little fox" of attraction and flirting grows into a big bad wolf of a full-fledged sexual affair.

The thing about little foxes is they eventually grow up to become Hungry Wolves that want to get fed, if they go unchecked. And when a Ravenous Wolf comes looking for something to sink its teeth into, you can best believe that it is going to devour the very fabric of your life until it destroys every good thing that you've been trying to CULTIVATE and PRODUCE.

And the thing about a little fox is, sometimes what looks like a little fox is really a BIG BAD WOLF in disguise. Now you may naively believe that you can handle a big bad wolf without getting eaten alive by it. You may even put an S on your chest and say…."Who's afraid of the big bad wolf?" But <u>Ephesians 4:27</u> warns us to not let the devil get a foothold. Because once he gets his foot in our hearts, minds and lives, his agenda is to devour anything and everything that is good and fruitful in our lives.

Likewise, if a farmer plants a field of corn and then gets invaded by field mice, it's hard to get the mice out once they're in because vermin breed quickly. Therefore, the farmer has to be diligent about monitoring his field so that the little rodents of life do not destroy the very thing that he is trying to cultivate and grow. The irony of it all is that a field mouse is miniscule in comparison to a vast corn field. However, we must always remember that it's not the size of the rodent that matters, it's their ability to spread and destroy what you're trying to build. And since the field mice's intent is to eat up all of your good fruit, you have to treat the field mice like the enemy to your field that it is. This very same principle applies to the little foxes that try to eat away at your fruitful thought life, fruitful faith, fruitful progress, fruitful purpose, fruitful gifts, fruitful habits, and fruitful relationships.

Our marching orders as duly noted in <u>Genesis 1:28</u> are.... "to be fruitful and multiply." But we cannot be fruitful and multiply if we are opening the gate to the little foxes in life that come to eat away at the precious things that we are trying to produce and cultivate. Remember to watch out for those little foxes, because little foxes eventually grow up to become big foxes with razor sharp teeth that have insatiable appetites that can ruin your vineyards while they're in bloom.

Just Like Every Dog Has Its Day... Every Goliath In Your Life Has A Slingshot Waiting For Him With His Name On It

By: Cassandra Mack

Sometimes life can hit you with a goliath of an issue that kicks you right in the middle of your and makes you question, if only for a moment, whether or not you're going to be able to make it. Has this ever happened to you?

Every human being on the planet has had times in their lives where they felt like the problem or problems that they were dealing with was so unrelenting and inescapable, that life seemed overwhelming and hopeless. And when your life is void of hope and it seems like your problems just won't let up, sometimes it can cause us to temporarily lose our way and contemplate doing something incredibly foolish or downright rash. I know because I have been there.... more than once.

The thing about goliaths is that they have a funny way of scaring the daylights out of us; similar to that imaginary monster who we believed was hiding under the bed waiting for our parents to turn out the lights so that they could grab us by the feet and get us.

Whether it's the monster of a job loss, money troubles, depression, loneliness, feelings of inadequacy, marriage problems, or your own children behaving in ways that create stress and drama ...when your problems won't let up; what starts off as a small issue hiding under the bed, if it goes unchecked eventually grows into a Goliath-level giant. And when the thing that's trying to come against you keeps lurking underneath your bed of your life, it can make you believe that you are less than a conqueror.

But here's what we learn about conquering the giants in our lives from 1 Samuel 17: 48 ... "As the Philistine moved closer to attack David, David ran quickly toward the battle line to meet Goliath."

This means that David faced his giant head on and did it quickly. David did not hesitate or sit around long enough to let self-doubt and fear overtake his mind. He faced the big problems in his life because he knew that with God on his side, he was more than a conqueror. Then we learn in 1 Samuel 17: 49 that "David reached into his bag and taking out a stone, he slung it and struck the Philistine on the forehead. The stone sank into his forehead, and he fell face down on the ground." This means that David had to reach down deep, to take out what was already in him, COURAGE, FAITH & THE PROMISES OF GOD, so that he could strike down the giant that was trying to defeat him and steal, kill and destroy his destiny.

Now here's where it gets so deep that if we are not paying close attention we may overlook the significance of it. In 1 Samuel 17: 51 we learn that..." David ran and stood over him. He took hold of the Philistine's sword and drew it from the sheath. After he killed him, he cut off his head with the sword."

The Soul Fast Workbook. Copyright © 2017 by Cassandra Mack.

Why is this important to remember? Because not only did David face his giant, no matter how seemingly big and scary; but after he conquered it, he stood over it just to let the enemy know who's boss and then cut the giant down to size by cutting off his head. Sometimes we have to cut an issue off by the head, to make sure that there's no life in it and that it is fully under our feet.

There are some Goliaths that you absolutely cannot afford to play around with like: the goliath of gambling, or an affair, or addictions ...so after you face it head on, you also have to make sure to cut it off at the head so that there is absolutely no strong holding power left in it.

So, what am I saying to you? Simply this: Whatever giant is trying to come against you to steal, kill and destroy your joy, purpose and destiny ...if you truly want to conquer it completely, then you've got to do what David did. Not only do you have to face your Goliath even if your emotions feel afraid, you've got to strike it down it, stand over it, take its weapons from it and cut it off at the head. Romans 8:37 tells us that we are more than conquerors. So, this means that no matter how challenging the road gets, no matter how intimidating your Goliaths may appear to be, you hold on and remember that if God is with you, then you've already got the victory ...because just like every dog has its day, every Goliath in your life has a slingshot with his name on it. Now go claim the victory!

Life Will Do You Like A Game of 3-Card Monte, Whenever You Hedge Your Bets From A Mindset of Deprivation

By: Cassandra Mack

When I was a teenager, in the 1980's my friends and I used to go to the movies and the arcades in Times Square in New York City. But back in the day, what is now known as Times Square used to be referred to as the 40-Deuce (don't judge the hood). The neighborhood was somewhat seedy back then, especially at night. In fact, 40-Deuce was a place that was saturated with pimps, prostitutes and con artists looking to run game on people and make a fast buck in the streets.

One of the games that was commonly played on the sidewalks of 40-Deuce was a card game known as 3 Card Monte. Tourists and native New Yorkers alike with an appetite for gambling, often fell victim to this scam of a game. But what they did not hedge their bets on was the fact that the game was a set up for them to lose their money from the get-go.

The people who played this game foolishly believed that they could out scam a seasoned scammer. But in reality, the game was a set up for failure. Why? Because you cannot out slick a slicker. It's kind of like dancing with the devil in your prettiest dress and expecting to come out of it unscathed. Just like there's no way in the world that you can dance with the devil without getting a little taste of hell, you cannot gamble away what's important to you without running the risk of losing the very thing that you value.

Now let's get back to the game. The most basic version of the 3 Card Monte card game involves two con artists: the inside man and the outside man. The outside man would find a Mark (*the person willing to bet their money)* pretend to befriend him and then bring the Mark into the card game which was run by the inside man. The outside man makes the Mark think that the two of them are united against the inside man who is tossing the card, when in reality the inside man and outside man are in cahoots with one another setting the mark up to get played. The outside man plays a few rounds and "wins" a little...at least that's how they make it seem to the Mark. And since the Mark thinks the game is a sure bet, he gambles his money away and ultimately loses. The mark mistakenly believes that he has figured out the card game, when in reality the two con artists saw the Mark coming from a mile away and set up the game from the very beginning for the Mark to lose all his money. And that's the game of 3 Card Monte.

Some of us play at life like a Mark in the game of 3 Card Monte. We hedge our bets on a temporary desire that is not in alignment with God's best for us, like: a tantalizing affair that that feels good while it's happening but that ultimately destroys your marriage, or spending out of control which makes you look like you got money when you're buying out the bar in the club but leaves you broke and bankrupt when it's time to pay the bill or making fast drug money in the streets at the risk of your life and freedom. See whenever we trade our destiny for a fleeting desire there's always a back-end consequence that will eventually show up to collect. Hosea 8:7 puts it this way...

"*The sow the wind and reap the whirlwind.*" Because the golden rule of life is this: We eventually reap what we sow.

Just like the Mark in the game of 3 Card Monte, when you give up your birthright, be it your birthright of (peace of mind, joy, a purpose-driven life) to quench a temporary fleeting thirst, you end up gambling away your destiny and blessings. And the craziest part of it all is we foolishly believe that we can outwit God and be successful doing it our way rather than God's way.

One of the first examples we see of this *3 Card Monte Mindset* is in the Biblical story of Jacob and Esau. In the story of Jacob and Esau found in Genesis 25: 27-34, it is noted that.... Jacob was "a quiet man, staying among the tents" and his mother's favorite, while Esau was "a skillful hunter, a man of the open country" and his father's favorite. One day, Esau returned from hunting and desired some of the lentil stew that Jacob was cooking. Jacob offered to give his brother some stew in exchange for his birthright—the special honor that Esau possessed as the oldest son, which gave him the right to a double portion of his father's inheritance. Esau put his temporary, physical desires over his God-given blessing and in the process ended up losing out on his birthright.

How many of us are like Esau, giving away what matters most or selling ourselves short to satisfy a fleeting desire? If we are honest, we've all had an Esau moment at some point in our lives. Whether you remained in a relationship with someone you did not love for financial reasons or some sort of personal gain, or hooked up with a married individual because you were lonely, horny and wounded or remained in a relationship with someone who did not value or respect you, because you didn't want to be alone ...and the list goes on.

See whenever we allow someone to steal God's best from us and take what's rightfully our right from under our nose, we are having an Esau moment. Whenever we make decisions from a place of deprivation or emotional thirst, we will always miss the mark, become the Mark and go into the situation with a losing hand. Each of us has had an Esau moment or maybe even an Esau season, so it's not about beating up on ourselves for making poor choices and having personal struggles, it's about doing our best each day to make better choices and not getting ahead of God's timing, even when we're really thirsty. Because when you make decisions while you are mentally or emotionally famished, you end up eating a stew that satisfies your flesh in the moment but that has far-reaching consequences that you will eventually have to pay.

So, remember, whenever you feel tempted to have an *Esau Moment* or resort to the *3 Card Monte Mentality*, the best way to ensure that you develop a winning hand is to let God do the guiding, leading and directing.

It's Never Too Late to Make A New Move

By: Cassandra Mack

One of my favorite dance songs is a song by the group Shalamar, titled "Make That Move." Now if you're old enough to remember anything about the group Shalamar, in the 1980's they put out hit song after hit of feel good R&B music. Whenever I play this song, I am reminded of the importance of knowing when to make new moves in our lives and when to do so swiftly.

Psalms 27: 14 tells us to... *"Wait on the LORD and be of good courage."* And without a doubt, God's timing is everything. But, 2 Samuel 5:24 says.... *"As soon as you hear the sound of marching in the tops of the poplar trees, move quickly, because that will mean the LORD has gone out in front of you to strike the Philistine army."*

So, what does this mean for us? Simply put it means this: There are times in our lives when God wants us to wait and then there are times in our lives when God has already given us the green light and we've got to move quickly in order to seize the moment. Why is it important to be able to differentiate between when God is speaking to you about exercising the virtue of patience as duly noted in Psalms 27:14 and when God is speaking to you about exercising the tactic of moving quickly as duly noted in 2 Samuel 5:34?

The reason that it's important to know the difference is because there are some opportunities that God needs us to wait on because we are still maturing in a particular area and the circumstances that He is orchestrating have not fully materialized yet. But on the flip side there are some opportunities that God has already gone before us and fully paved the way for and He is waiting for us to walk boldly into our destiny. Where can it be said in your life that it's time to...*Make That Move Right Now?*

- Do you need to move quickly on an idea that has been percolating inside your head?
- Do you need to move quickly on a project at work or a new venture in your business?
- Do you need to move forward on your plans to go back to school or write that book or record your music and sell it yourself through an online outlet?
- Do you need to make some different moves in your finances?
- Do you need to move away from some people and do so swiftly because they are holding you back?

As you consider these questions, I'll leave you with a verse from the song *"Make That Move"* ...

So many times, by holding back I let the good things pass me by
And then one day I asked myself the reason why
And like an answer from above you came into my life.
Make that move right now, baby
You only go out once in a lifetime
Make that move right now, baby

Fruit Bowls and Fruitcakes: The Reason Why No One Really Gets You

By: Cassandra Mack

One of the hardest life lessons to come to terms with is knowing that more often than not, YOU won't fit in. There will be a clique who does not embrace you, a group who does not want you in their little circle and people that you know in passing who will not celebrate you or receive you with love and even those who may blatantly reject you in the meanest of ways. But here is where you have to know the difference between fruit bowls and fruit cakes. Fruit bowls are meant to please everybody therefore they can never stand out. But fruitcakes are only for those with a big enough palate to appreciate them. And even if you are not that partial to the taste of fruitcake, you can certainly appreciate the uniqueness and flavor of them.

When no matter where you go or who you're with, there is always something about you that is a little different, it can make you want to jump in the fruit bowl with the apples and oranges when you were meant to be a fruitcake that is so fearfully and wonderfully made that it is truly something to be marveled at. When your mindset is God-centered, and the manner in which you move through the world is one where the things of God are important to you, you simply will not blend in with the fruit the neatly fit in the fruit bowl. Instead your vibe will be more like that of a fruitcake – special, beautiful, full of flavor and glorious. There is nothing wrong with you!

So, if you always feel felt like you are the odd guy or odd girl out, the strange bird in the flock that nobody truly understands, it's because fruitcakes are not meant to fit into fruit bowls, they are meant to be presented on cake stands. There has never been another YOU before and there will never be another YOU again in life. That's why, the people who you meet, work with and even some of the people in your family may not always thoroughly get YOU, because there are too many intricacies that make you uniquely YOU for someone else to fully understand.

Even in nature, you can compare a Macintosh apple to a Red Delicious or a California grown orange with a Florida grown one. But who can really and truly compare to YOU? No one can. Even if there is somebody else with similar traits, characteristics and a comparable temperament, there has still never been and there never will be another YOU in life. You are a unique one of a kind Soul with your own thoughts, experiences ad feelings. Therefore, no one will ever completely grasp everything about you that makes you uniquely, except The One who created you.

One of Shakespeare's most famous quotes is..." This *above all: to thine own self be true.*" But you can't be true to yourself, unless you are comfortable being everything that God created and purposed you to be. Everyone goes through seasons in their lives where they feel alienated and misunderstood. And sometimes in an effort to fit in the fruit bowl, we try to become someone that we are not. Now granted, at times it can seem easier to fit in with the crowd than to stand in the truth of who YOU are and risk being the odd man out. But the bigger reality of your life is that you were set apart for a special purpose.

The Soul Fast Workbook. Copyright © 2017 by Cassandra Mack.

<u>1 Peter 2: 9</u> tells us this: *"But ye are a chosen generation, a royal priesthood, a holy nation, a peculiar people; that ye should shew forth the praises of him who hath called you out of darkness into his marvelous light."*

The bible reminds us that we as Believers are a peculiar people. And although in the natural, being viewed as peculiar might make you feel like you're weird or bizarre. However, one of the definitions for the word peculiar is - *belonging exclusively to*. And when you belong exclusively to God, you will begin to do things that are atypical, unexpected, and uncharacteristic of the way that most people do things.

The word "peculiar" comes from the Latin word *Peculium*, which means private property. When you are God's private property, you will begin to behave in ways that will both astound and dumbfound people, because the behavior within itself is so atypical of how most people would respond if they were in the same situation.

Here are some examples of peculiar behavior that you may find yourself doing if you are a new creature in Christ.

✓ Somebody can say something to make you want to curse them out or beat the stupidity right out of them, but instead of getting pulled into their negativity, you decide to keep your composure and possibly even pray for them.

✓ Or, you find out from a mutual friend that another friend is talking trash about you, and instead of calling them up and telling them to keep your name out of their mouth or else... you let it go and pray for their growth.

✓ Or, you find that you would be well within your rights to exercise a little payback to someone who had it coming, but instead of serving their head on a silver platter, you choose to show them the kind of mercy that they did not show you.

Now if this type of behavior is not peculiar, I don't know what is. Speaking for myself, I find it extremely peculiar that lately whenever somebody does something that I find incredibly annoying, God gives me the strength to let it go. You are empowered with this same strength of spirit. This strength of spirit is noted in <u>2 Timothy 1:7</u> *"For God hath not given us the spirit of fear, but of power and of love and of a sound mind."*

So today, know that it's okay if you're a little peculiar and if you dance to a different beat. Because when there's music in your soul otherwise known as the joy of The Lord and a rhythm in your life known as faith, not only does it change how you do things, but it also changes your outlook and your heart. Bon appetite'.

Productive Relationships Are Always Based On Shared Purpose & Agreement

In order for our relationships to be HEALTHY and PRODUCTIVE they must have two important elements: SHARED PURPOSE and AGREEMENT. This principle of PURPOSE and AGREEMENT is so critical to our very existence that even in human anatomy, we learn that the right connection of atoms at the most finite level of life are essential to the growth and health of every system in the body. If one single cell strays from its purpose, or if the nervous system decides it doesn't want to work with the circulatory system or if the wrong proton attaches itself to the wrong neutron; the whole body is out of alignment and at greater risk for Dis-EASE and DEATH. In fact, if one biological system decides that it does not want to work together cohesively with the rest of the systems in the body, the entire body will shut down and die a slow debilitating death. Why? Because they are not working together in agreement.

Sometimes we hold on to relationships that are dying a slow and debilitating death when God is telling us to move forward in purpose and let the dead bury the dead (Luke 9:60). Unhealthy connections whether in the friendship realm, the intimate relationship realm or the sub-atomic unseen realm of our physical anatomy will always bring about cancerous conditions and dis-ease of the heart, unless we make the choice to let go of the people, places and things who are not being fruitful or multiplying the wellbeing and productivity in our lives.

Sometimes the reason why WE EXPERIENCE EMOTIONAL CANCER whenever we are in the vicinity of certain people or we become inflicted with a feeling of DIS-EASE in our soul that keeps resurfacing when we think of certain people is because we have allowed ourselves to remain emotionally attached to people who are no longer right for the season we're moving in and who do not have a clear purpose in our lives, so they begin to create disharmony and strife.

In human biology, even a white blood cell knows when it's time to stop hanging on to a red blood cell and cease fighting a dis-ease because it's time to completely let go. Know that sometimes in life, in order to experience the full fruit of your next season you will be required to let go OF some of the people and things in your life that are not MULTIPLYING YOUR PEACE, PROSPERITY and JOY and who are simply not producing good fruit in your life.

The Soul Fast Workbook. Copyright © 2017 by Cassandra Mack.

Don't Get Caught In Hard To Walk Places Wearing A Pair of Flip Flops.

About six few years ago, there was a malfunction within the subway system in New York City that required riders to get off the train and walk through the tunnel as directed by the Mass Transit Authority personnel. And if you were there and you were looking at the subway tracks, you couldn't help but notice that there were quite a few flip flop sandals that got caught in the tracks. This meant that there were some people who had lost one or both of their foot coverings and had to walk through the dark and filthy subway tunnel either barefoot or with just one flip flop on. The thing about Flip Flops is this: They are not built to endure too much pressure on the feet nor are they sturdy enough to WITHSTAND a long WALK in dark, difficult places. So it is not wise to wear flip flop sandals when you are traveling underground or if there is even the slightest risk that you may have to walk in a dark or uncomfortable place.

The thing about it is, the people who lost their flip flops had their feet exposed to all kinds of debris, dangerous metal, flammable trash, rats, exposed needles and every other disease carrying thing that was on the subway tracks. However, the people whose FEET were FULLY COVERED like those who had on closed toed shoes and sneakers were protected from most of the resulting debris.

Isn't it ironic that when your FEET are covered, you don't suffer nearly as much collateral damage as when your feet are exposed to toxins and trash? The simple answer is flip flops are not made for long distance walking or for walking in hard places.

Did you know that your thought life works in a similar fashion? Whenever we have *Flip Flop Faith*, rather than Mustard Seed Faith which comes by hearing the Word of God, it becomes increasingly difficult to keep on walking even when you have to walk in dark places. But when we build our faith and put on the full armor of God each morning our feet are better protected because we have our spiritual shoes on which is the Gospel of Peace. But when we don't get dressed properly in the spirit, we become more prone to being hit by Enemies like: Depression, Feeling of Inadequacy or Doubt which tend to engulf us with psychological debris so that they can grab us by the FEET and HINDER Our WALK.

Now before you think that I have completely lost my mind and my wits, let me tell you why I believe this to be true. The bible tells us to put on the Full Armor of God Ephesians 6:10- 18. The 3rd piece of armor that we are told to put on are the "SHOES OF THE GOSPEL OF PEACE."

Consequently, the number "3" is the number of ascension which for us as humans is the ability to rise in the spirit, from the realm of death (depression is a form of death as it kills your joy, stability, emotional equilibrium and peace of mind) into the realm of life (where you experience greater peace, joy and emotional equilibrium) So it's no accident that the 3rd piece of spiritual armor are the Shoes of the Gospel of PEACE.

Secondly, your shoes go on your feet. Now your FEET represent your ability to MOVE from dead places to life-affirming places, to MOVE from any place that God tells you to move from shaking the dust off your feet so that you can MOVE into the place that God wants you to GO. Your FEET enable you to STAND on God's Word in mind, body and spirit and to stand firmly on each and every one of God's promises.

Your FEET stir you to be MOVED by the Holy Spirit and take a LEAP of FAITH even if your faith is at the mustard-seed level of development. Your FEET provide you with the POWER, RESILIENCE, STRENGTH, MOBILITY and ABILITY to WALK out your faith one STEP at a time so that you can do like the gospel duo, Mary Mary sings about and ...GO GET YOUR BLESSINGS ...which includes the blessing of your Peace that surpasses all understanding, your ability to walk in PURPOSE and DESTINY despite your circumstances and your ability to kick down or maneuver around the obstacles in your path so that you can SEIZE Your SUCCESS.

So surely if you can STEP IN THE NAME of LOVE. you can WALK in the NAME OF Your PURPOSE, PEACE and SOUNDNESS OF MIND.

See because the enemy knows that as long he's keeps you in Flip Flops, when the time comes to walk in dark places he will have you by the FEET. And when the enemy has you by the feet, he can keep you immobilized and stagnant, he can counsel your mind and keep you seated in a bed of depression by or unforgiveness. But your life doesn't have to be this way. You do have a choice. You don't have to let the enemy win. You can choose to put away the Flip Flops, Cover Your Feet and take authority over your life by GETTING UP and WALKING this thing out, until you get to your faith-filled place of peace of mind.

When your FEET are COVERED with the GOSPEL OF PEACE, you become empowered to move yourself mentally from one place to another by the renewing of your mind with prayer and scripture. You become empowered to move yourself emotionally from one place to another by praying God's word which gives you the power to do three things: STEP BACK to get clarity, STEP AWAY FROM the distractions to have some alone time with God and STEP INTO new perspectives, new mindsets and new realms of peace and personal power through Christ who gives us the strength to do all things.

So know that although depression enters in through the mind gate (Our Thoughts) and ear gate (what we listen to repeatedly), it GRIPS US by the FEET through stagnation.

So today, if you are feeling discouraged, put away your flip flops and cover your FEET with the WORD OF GOD so that when life requires you to walk in hard-to-walk places you can do so with resilience and hope. And know that no matter what it looks like in the natural, with God on your side, you have the power to put one foot in front of the other and WALK.

Have you been thinking about gathering with a group of friends in your home or meeting up with other members of your church so that you can do the soul fast as a group? Know that if God is leading you to start a Soul Fast Group then it can be done. If you have a heart for people and a sincere interest in leading a Soul Fast Group, below are some tips to help you start your group.

A Soul Fast Group is an empowering and supportive way for people to: fast as a community while enjoying fresh fellowship, keep themselves accountable to their commitment to do the Soul Fast, lift each other up in prayer; as well as build authentic relationships with like-minded people who want to grow in their faith.

The key to developing a successful Soul Fast group is to create the kind of atmosphere and group dynamics where people feel embraced and that grows out of an authentic commitment to support one another in their Soul Fast journey. Following are 10 simple tips to help you get started.

1. Pray About It

I know it seems obvious but take some time to pray. Pray that God give you everything you need to lead a successful soul fast group. Ask God to draw you to the people that should be part of your group. Perhaps you already have some people in mind that you would like to invite to do the soul fast as a group or maybe you'll be reaching out to people one by one as God leads you. Although you might not know their names yet, God does, so pray about all of the details concerning the people that He will draw to your group and the group logistics. Consider asking a group of prayer warriors or even one other praying person to pray specifically for this group that God has placed on your heart and watch God bring together everything you need for starting your Soul Fast Group.

2. Keep The Overall Purpose In Mind

The purpose of these meetings would be to gather people together who have agreed to do this Soul Fast as a group to have a safe place to talk about the issues that they are struggling with and the goals that they are striving toward as they embark on the 40-day Soul Fast journey. Essentially, the Soul Fast Group would be a meeting place to talk about and pray about the issues, breakthroughs and ah ha moments that come up for people as they do this soul fast.

3. Write Your Vision & Make It Plain

What is your vision for this Soul Fast Group that you want to host? See your vision in your mind's eye and then write it down in 2 or 3 sentences. A vision helps focus your efforts in one direction so that when you invite people to be part of your Soul Fast Group, you can clearly communicate what you're seeking to do and why rather than rambling off in multiple directions. When you invite people to be part of your Soul Fast group, you should be able to tell them in a few words what you're trying to do and why you think they will benefit by being part of it.

4. Think About Who You're Trying To Reach

Who do you already know that you think would want to do the Soul Fast with you? Start there! Are there women, men or parents who need a supportive community where they can fellowship and the soul fast group that you want to host would be a great place to meet them right where they're at? Can you reach out to people in a place where people already congregate like a coffee shop, a business or Zumba class or even your local laundry mat? Will you reach out to neighbors, family members, seniors, friends, co-workers, members of your church, members of an online community that you already are a part of, women only, men only, mothers and daughters, fathers and sons, single parents, people in recovery, couples? The more targeted your group is, the more you'll find that people will be drawn to your group. Not only that, people will be more likely to open up during the group meetings and share their struggles, progress, hopes and goals, because they will feel comfortable knowing that the group is not only designed to help them grow spiritually as they embark on the soul fast journey together, but additionally the group will be a place that speaks to where they are practically because they will have the added benefit of common interests, priorities and challenges.

5. Select A Regular Meeting Location and Time

Where will you meet? Will you meet in your home, alternate between different group members homes or in a public place like a café or library? Try to make your meeting space as welcoming and comfortable as possible. Ideally your group should meet once a week for 6 to 8 weeks. Will you meet for an hour, 90-minutes or two hours? Decide on a meeting location, day of the week and meeting length.

6. Establish Expectations

For your group to run smoothly people need to know what to expect and what is expected of them. You need to establish some basic ground rules around how the meetings will run, how people ought to conduct themselves during the meetings, how members ought to treat each other as well as the importance of not gossiping about what is shared during the meetings, so that the group is a safe space to lift burdens, pray for one another and be encouraged.

7. Allow For The Group To Be Interactive

Facilitate the group without monopolizing it. Allow conversations to flow among the group once you've introduced a topic or asked a conversation-starter question. Your role as host and facilitator is to set up the meetings, listen for the needs, welcome people into the group and set the tone that everyone's voice matters and that you're in this journey together. This encourages people to make the group their own. Also, every now and then you can incorporate an icebreaker activity that breaks the ice and ties in with the theme of the meeting on that particular day. Or you can ask another group member to lead an icebreaker activity. You can also plan to have refreshments or ask everyone to bring a dish to provide an opportunity for group members to fellowship casually.

The Soul Fast Workbook. Copyright © 2017 by Cassandra Mack.

8. Remember It's Their Group Too

Your group members have valuable gifts and helpful information to share. Ask them for their ideas and input. And if it aligns with your purpose and vision for the group, you can incorporate it into your meetings.

9. Plan Your Agenda

By the first meeting you want to make sure that everyone has purchased their copy of *The Soul Fast Workbook*. During the meetings, your discussion topics should align with the 4 sections of *The Soul Fast Workbook*. For example, if your Soul Fast Group is going to run for 6 to 8 weeks you can follow these suggested steps:

- As people are coming in, you introduce group members to each other and allow about 15 minutes for casual socializing and refreshments. Have extra pens available.
- Always start and end each meeting with prayer.
- The 1st meeting might focus on each member discussing the reason that they've decided to join your Soul Fast Group, what they hope to receive and achieve by going on this soul fast, (Is it clarity about a decision they need to make, a breakthrough in a particular area of their lives, emotional healing, a more productive mindset, or something else?) and what they hope to get from the Soul fast group experience.
- The 2nd meeting should focus on section 1 of The Soul Fast Workbook, which deals with The Mind. You can talk about the work you completed using the daily worksheets in this section and what this process was like for you. Talk about what you learned, any breakthroughs you had, any challenges you've experienced and the progress that you are making by sticking with the soul fast.
- The 3rd meeting should focus on section 2 of The Soul Fast Workbook, which deals with The Heart. You can talk about the work you completed using the daily worksheets in this section and what this process was like for you. Talk about what you learned, any breakthroughs you had, any challenges you've experienced and the progress that you are making by sticking with the soul fast.
- The 4th meeting should focus on section 3 of The Soul Fast Workbook, which deals with The Will. You can talk about the work you completed using the daily worksheets in this section and what this process was like for you. Talk about what you learned, any breakthroughs you had, any challenges you've experienced and the progress that you are making by sticking with the soul fast.
- The 5th meeting should focus on section 4 of The Soul Fast Workbook, which deals with Relationships. You can talk about the work you completed using the daily worksheets in this section and what this process was like for you. Talk about what you learned, any breakthroughs you had, any challenges you've experienced and the progress that you are making by sticking with the soul fast.
- The 6th meeting should be a celebration of your culmination of The Soul Fast Workbook as a group. Or perhaps the group has decided to meet for an additional week or two in order to have more time to talk about the 4 sections of the workbook and the resulting issues that came up for each of you. If this is your last meeting, talk about what the overall process was like for you. Talk about what you learned and gained by embarking on this Soul Fast journey together. Talk about what you learned

The Soul Fast Workbook. Copyright © 2017 by Cassandra Mack.

from one another as well as the ways in which participating in this Soul Fast group has changed your life.

10. Determine What's Next.

At the last scheduled meeting, you may find that the group wants to continue meeting. Perhaps you now want to focus on studying the bible together or doing some sort of pay-it-forward project as a group. Or, perhaps you want to start another Soul Fast Group with a whole new group of people. Whatever you decide, pray on it and let God direct your path.

11. Consider Starting Your Own Facebook Group

If your group members are already using Facebook, you might want to create a private Facebook group for your soul fast group. A Facebook page can be a great communication tool to keep a conversation going in between meetings, post updates, prepare your key meeting points before the actual meeting or ask relevant questions that group members can respond to in the comments section of a post. You can even do a Facebook live video where you and other group members can interact with one another live online. If ever you want to expand your group, simply invite people from your friends list and encourage others to invite their friends and your group will grow.

12. Consider Doing An Abridged Soul Fast Group Focusing On Just One of The Areas In The Soul Fast Workbook

When your original soul fast group has ended, why not start another soul group where you do an abbreviated version of the soul fast. Perhaps you want to go even deeper with detoxing from unhealthy thinking and self-talk so that you can build better confidence and stronger self-esteem. Since section 1 of *The Soul Fast Workbook* focuses on fasting from toxic thoughts, mindsets and self-talk, when your first round of the Soul Fast Group comes to an end, you can start another group where you fast from toxic words and invite new members to join you. You can create a Facebook page for your group and set up a designated time for 10 days in a row where everyone joins the conversation online or you can use a free conference call service and meet by phone. Group members would do the daily worksheets in section 1 of *The Soul Fast Workbook,* and then post a question, bible verse or meme around how to change self-defeating thoughts to self-empowering ones for 10 days in a row and have group members respond to the posts. Group members would commit to fasting from negative thinking and self-talk for 10 days in a row, they would do the daily worksheets in section 1 of the workbook and you would meet online each day of the mini soul fast to support and encourage one another in whichever particular area that you decided to focus on as a group. Since everyone may not be in the same place with respect to their faith journey, an abridged Soul Fast Group works well for people who are not yet ready to commit to an entire 40-day fast but, will be open to the process of a soul fast if they can take it in pieces without any pressure.

Sign Up For Life Coaching with Cassandra Mack

Whenever we step into a new season of life, or move into higher realms of responsibility or we want to experience greater success and effectiveness in a particular area of our lives; we must develop new tools, skills and strategies to take us where we want to go. When we have the right knowledge, the right framework, the right strategies and the right tools we become empowered to achieve our goals with greater ease and we are better prepared to step into the task that we are about to embark on with clarity confidence and competence.

The real value of being in a coaching relationship with a life coach who is bible-based is twofold: First, the Bible is the primary framework that undergirds the coaching sessions. Second the tips, tools and tactics that we will utilize together will be in alignment with your foundational beliefs and faith.

Whether you want to focus on leadership development, your relationships or your emotional well-being, coaching with Cassandra Mack will help you get unstuck, create a sustainable plan to help you achieve your desired results and provide you with strategies to move your life in the direction that you want to go in with greater clarity, confidence, and effectiveness.

What makes coaching with Cassandra Mack, exceptionally beneficial is, Cassandra bridges the psychology of success, the dynamics of human behavior, and timeless Biblical principles with her innovative empowerment strategies and 17 plus years of successful experience as an executive coach, master facilitator, social worker and thought leader to help individuals and organization build capacity and enhance wellbeing. As a result, Cassandra Mack offers her clients a deeper understanding of what's driving their behavior, what's hindering their success and how to tap their inner strengths and unrealized potential which in turn enables them to achieve their goals faster and utilize her unique techniques to make their lives better.

Are you ready to live a more inspired, and intentional life? Try a coaching session with Cassandra Mack and start seizing your success and repositioning yourself for victorious living.
KingdomKeysWithCassandraMack.com

7 Benefits to Bringing A Cassandra Mack Professional Development Training to Your Organization

Are you an HR Director or executive facing an organizational or employee challenge within your company that needs to be addressed and explored? Cassandra Mack has helped hundreds of individuals, nonprofit organizations and government agencies develop effective ways to deal with workplace issues that impact performance and productivity. Executives, HR and Organizational Development directors have used Cassandra Mack to tackle some of the most common challenges that plague work environments, such as:

- Ineffective or toxic communication
- Low team morale or staff burnout
- Conflict avoidance and non-resolution
- Lack of productivity and interpersonal agility
- Misalignment about roles on a team
- Leading others towards their best success
- How to coach, counsel and mentor employees for maximum productivity

From leadership development for your executive level managers and supervisory skills for new supervisors to professionalism and personal effectiveness for your entire team; Cassandra Mack can work with your organization to help you achieve your desired results. Whether you want to maximize the diverse gifts and talents of your leaders; equip your front-line staff with the essential skills to align with vision, build team cohesion, communicate better, boost morale or adapt well to new changes, Cassandra Mack can assist you. Cassandra Mack's educational courses and professional development learning programs will help you reach your goals faster and empower your staff to do their jobs with greater skill, ease and effectiveness. Below are **7 Benefits** to bringing a Cassandra Mack Training Program to your organization:

1. Increase the collective knowledge of your entire team when they have vastly different viewpoints and work styles that hinder staff alignment and team cohesion.

2. Help your employees function better interpersonally so that managers spend less time refereeing conflicts and miscommunication and more time maximizing their team members and resources.

3. Groom future leaders for your organization. When a manager leaves the company, there is often a decline in productivity due to the company not being able to fill the position with a qualified candidate. But with targeted training now, you can help ensure your current workforce is prepared to seamlessly move up the ladder as needed.

4. Enable managers/supervisors to develop a better assessment of their employees' strengths, professional goals and developmental needs consequently maximizing employee retention and growth.

5. Better prepare your employees to develop interpersonal agility skills in order to deal with the changing demands of the workplace and business environment.

6. Align employees conduct, work habits and professional practices with the culture, mission and vision of your organization as well as the goals of each department within your company.

7. Make it easier for your organization to know where to plan, budget and allocate resources by evaluating the outcome of the training.

➤ For more information about **Cassandra Mack's Workplace Training Programs**, go to: StrategiesForEmpoweredLiving.com

The Soul Fast Workbook. Copyright © 2017 by Cassandra Mack.

Other Books by Cassandra Mack

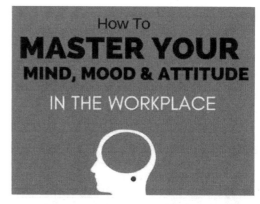